Aftermath

SURVIVE

AND

OVERCOME

TRAUMA

Mariann Hybels-Steer, Ph.D.

A FIRESIDE BOOK
PUBLISHED BY SIMON & SCHUSTER
New York London Toronto
Sydney Tokyo Singapore

FIRESIDE
Rockefeller Center
1230 Avenue of the Americas
New York, New York 10020

Designed by Crowded House Design

Manufactured in the United States of America

10   9   8   7   6   5   4   3   2   1

Library of Congress Cataloging-in-Publication Data

Hybels-Steer, Mariann.
    Aftermath : survive and overcome trauma / Mariann Hybels-Steer.
        p.   cm.
    "A Fireside book."
    Includes bibliographical references and index.
    1. Post-traumatic stress disorder—Popular works.   2. Psychic
trauma.   I. Title.
    RC552.P67H93   1995
    616.85'21—dc20   94-35188
                                                                  CIP

ISBN: 0-671-88389-5

To
TRM,
The love of my life
and
DLM,
A friend unsurpassed

Acknowledgments

Because a book reflects a lifetime of exposure to the work, writing, and experience of others blended with one's own work, writing, and experience, I could not begin to acknowledge everyone who helped author this book; therefore, I must limit myself to those who were the most influential.

Believe it or not, the person in my most distant past that I would like to thank is my third grade teacher! She was the first to suggest I had some talent for writing after I had submitted a one-page paper on Paul Bunyan. It's amazing how much mileage a kid can get from one person's brief recognition. Also, from years past (as well as from now), my Aunt Jean for simply loving me.

More currently, I would like to thank Dr. Judy Welles, who saw something in me before I could imagine it, and Dr. Leonard Felder, who guided me through many of the steps of launching this project. I also want to thank Carol Mann, my agent, who understood both my idea for the book and my belief it had to be written in an easy-to-read format, and Sheila

M. Curry who made my first foray into working with an editor as easy as it could be. And to those who gave hours of time by doing the grunt work of reading, editing, and word processing: Dr. Diane Mink, Tom Miller, Lauri Maerov, Dr. Michael Diamond, Linda Ludwig, and Cindy Miller. Thanks also to Ty, Ryan, and Amy Miller who embraced me and, without knowing it, eased a deep pain. And, of course, to everyone who made themselves available to be interviewed for this book, for you brought your experiences out to be viewed in order to aid and comfort others who have had similar traumas. I learned something new from each of you.

Contents

Part Three
The Middle Period of Disarray

Part Four
Putting It into Place via Resolution

Part Five
For Those Close to Someone Traumatized

Part Six
Traumatized Children

Part Seven
When Someone Dies

Part Eight
Final Thoughts

Appendices

Foreword

This book is written for easy use.

I have written this book in an easy-to-read format. This is because almost everyone who goes through a trauma **cannot concentrate and cannot process complex information.** In fact, these are two of the first signs that someone is experiencing a post-trauma reaction. Something seems to happen to our brains following trauma. It isn't that we've become stupid—it's as if we become frazzled. Frazzled brains can't make much sense out of long paragraphs with complex sentences. Once you have read the introduction, you've read the most complex part of this book. Other than the personal vignettes about people who have experienced trauma, the book is written in bite-size pieces. **The statements are short but meaty, and the book is organized by sections; therefore, you have to read only what is relevant to you at the time.**

I have included the **personal stories of others** who have gone through trauma. For some, the trauma happened a short time ago; for others, it has been years. A variety of traumatic events will be touched upon in these personal stories. For example, for one person it was a blinding gunshot wound; for another, an earthquake; for still another, a bicycle accident. Whatever the trauma, knowing about others who have shared similar experiences can often be the most helpful tool in healing. As you hear the words of others, I believe you will find your experience over and over again. You will hear yourself in these voices of shock, disbelief, helplessness, courage, pain, astonishment, anguish, rage, perplexity, hope, resentment, sadness, peace, perseverance, social action, and opportunity. You will hear—and you will recover, as they did.

PART ONE

Introduction

---

*What happens in life
really isn't very important . . .
how you react to it is.*

CHAPTER ONE

The Author's Story

It was a cold but clear February day in Michigan when it happened. I was in a quiet, well-kept suburb in an area called Downriver Detroit. Looking for a particular address, I was preoccupied when I made the right-hand turn that proved to be life-altering.

Before I realized what was happening, my car was surrounded by a mob of high school–age rioters incensed by the actions earlier that day of school board members who had removed posters of coveted, radical leaders. They were on a rampage and I was the first moving target they encountered. Their rage was blind, so it didn't matter that I, personally, wasn't the object of their anger.

I was pulled out of my car and onto the pavement. My car high-idled itself into a tree. I felt the rising terror. I felt the boots and shoes against my legs, my back, my shoulders, pounding at me through my heavy winter clothing. But, worse, I felt the blows against my unprotected head.

A coldness overtook me. In an instant I had become nothing and could do nothing. I don't know how many there were, but there were a lot. The street and the walkways were filled. Even if I could have gotten up from the relentless beating, I couldn't have gotten away.

I don't know how long it lasted. It seemed fast. It seemed slow. It seemed like the blink of an eye. It seemed like an eternity. Time compressed. Time elongated.

I heard a voice above me—a voice calling out to the others, telling them not to hurt me, telling them I had nothing to do with what they were angry about. I couldn't really see him, but I could hear him and I knew he was the only one trying to help and that he was as alone as I was. I was heartened by his effort to stand up to his peers, to fight a battle most wouldn't dare take on. They didn't listen to him. His objections didn't stop their assaults, but his effort and his presence calmed me, giving me hope and making me feel like I was more than nothing.

On the other side of the rioters, but unknown to me, was a patrol car. It was attempting to disperse the crowd by following them slowly with bullhorned messages. When they saw something was happening, they left their car and broke through the crowd. Their presence was sensed quickly by the mob, and the boot and shoe kicks stopped as quickly as they had begun. The young boy who had tried to help me leaned down and put his arms under my own to lift me up from the pavement. Our eyes met for only as long as he dared to stay. I don't know if it was time enough for him to see my gratitude.

I was being jostled around as the rioters broke apart running in all directions to avoid arrest and the police were running in all directions to make arrests. I was bewildered and stunned and disarmed by my inability to think. I just stood there being jostled. It seemed everything was happening backwards. It seemed as if someone should be asking about me or helping me, but I was lost in all the commotion. When I was found, it was by the irate homeowner whose fence and tree had been damaged by my car, blaming me, yelling at me. When the emergency team arrived it was the fire department, with no medical team. When I was questioned by the authorities, the questions were about what happened and not about how I was. When I was finally taken to a nearby police station, I called a family member, who arrived quickly. But rather than being helpful, he became hysterical. And, still, no one asked how I was. I guess because I looked unhurt, no one figured there was any need to ask. I was dismissed after the paperwork was completed and the administrative questions were answered.

The fact was, I wasn't unhurt. Because the initial shock left me numb, the injuries took some time to reveal themselves. I spent that first night in a stunned, robotic state. I also spent it on my studio couch in the living room, where I ended up spending many nights for a long time after. A bedroom with no door to the outside was, in my mind, a place with no escape. I wanted no part of such a place again.

The next morning, although still in shock emotionally, my body was no longer numb. And without the numbness, I discovered there wasn't a place on my body that didn't hurt. I reexperienced every boot and shoe kick in each attempt to move. And then days later, after I was able to move more freely, I realized I couldn't maintain my balance. A trip to the doctor revealed inner ear damage that would force me onto disability and a six-month period of being unable to drive or work.

It was during this period that I began to crawl inside myself. There was no one with whom I could talk. I felt isolated in a world of shock and pain and fear. It was probably the loneliest time in my life. I was alienated from myself because I couldn't feel anything, and I was alienated from others because no one knew what I was experiencing and no one knew how to ask. There were many people in my life, including my husband, but they were going about their normal lives while I was having an inexplicable and abnormal experience. In many ways, the loneliness was the worst part of the recovery. I was isolated in a world of confusion and fear, left stranded and feeling crazy.

Weeks later an incident occurred that made me fear I really

had gone off the deep end. I answered a knock at the door to find a black boy no more than ten years of age. He was selling chocolate bars. In response to his skin color—the same as the rioters—I felt the terror rise up. I slammed the door in his expectant young face and broke into uncontrollable sobs. I was sure I had gone crazy. I had gone from being able to work on a daily basis to being a hysterical puddle who sobbed uncontrollably, who couldn't leave her own apartment without an escort, who couldn't work, and who, for months, couldn't be in a crowd without panicking. I could attribute some of my reactions to the physical injuries, but they seemed minor compared to the damage to my psyche. But crazy? Now I understand I wasn't crazy. I was reacting unusually, yes, but it was a normal reaction given what I had gone through.

This book is about what happens in the aftermath. I wrote this book because no one knew how to help me. I didn't know that I was experiencing normal and predictable aftereffects that had a life of their own. I didn't know there was a beginning and a middle and an end to what I was experiencing. And I didn't know that the end included its never being completely over.

It is now twenty-three years later, and The-Day-I-Was-Beaten-up-in-the-Riot still lives with me. It doesn't debilitate me, but it does make me more careful than most. I feel a ribbon of fear whenever I am alone in the street and I see a group walking toward me. I *always* cross over to the other side, *always*. And the day I watched Reginald Denny pulled from his truck and beaten in the Los Angeles riots, I had repetitive flashes of The-Day-I-Was-Beaten-up-in-the-Riot interrupt my viewing of the footage of his horror, transporting me to another place and time.

I'm all right now. I know something that others who have not yet experienced trauma cannot know. I know that when something unexpected, frightening, and life-altering happens, I can survive. I know, most importantly, that I am more than the event—that I am not defined by the trauma but, instead, that the trauma is just one moment in the experience of my life.

From the Personal to the Professional

Given my own trauma, I guess it shouldn't have come as a surprise that as I pursued my advanced degree in psychology I developed a specialization in treating people who had experienced one-time trauma, as well as repetitive trauma. I began the professional leg of this journey in 1976. Since that time, I have studied the work of others, have written, and have lectured about trauma. During these years, almost all of my clients have been exposed to various types of trauma, ranging from moderate to severe.

In the last twenty years, much has been learned about sudden trauma. Now, we can provide victims with a clear understanding of the process of recovery. One of the things we have learned is that it is helpful for you to know that what you are experiencing is predictable and understandable. We have also learned that knowing what to expect in the aftermath can be most helpful to a full recovery. And finally, knowing and hearing about the experiences of others is not only reassuring but also accelerates recovery. This book brings you all of this in the hope that your progress will be made easier and will occur as quickly as possible.

CHAPTER TWO

Does Trauma Apply to You?

Is this book for you?

- This book is for you if you have experienced a one-time, sudden, and potentially life-threatening event. This could be anything from a near-fatal shooting to a tornado to an auto accident.

- This book is for you if you have experienced such an event and it has left you feeling and behaving differently from how you felt and behaved before. This difference may be obvious or it may be subtle. It's obvious when you're crying all the time, can't sleep, and/or can't work or concentrate. However, for some of you it may take weeks, even months, before you realize you've changed. You may be more irritable or less patient or keep forgetting things. You may not even realize you've been affected until you read this book. The degree of the effect is different for different people. Your reaction depends on many variables. For instance:
  - How frightening the event was.
  - How intense the event was.
  - How long the event lasted.
  - How you were doing before the event.

- This book is for you if you have been traumatized.

What Is a Trauma?

- A trauma is . . .
  - Something that makes you realize you could have died.
  - Something that makes you feel powerless, helpless, and paralyzed.
  - Sudden and overwhelming. It owns you, you don't own it.
  - A time when you experience extreme fear, even if only for a short while.
  - A time when you cannot think clearly.
  - More than stress. Stress does not have the sudden and life-threatening quality that trauma has.
  - A shock to the system, which is why it affects the **whole** system and creates a state of emergency.
  - An event with a predictable aftermath.

If It Doesn't Show, How Come It Hurts?

- You still may be wondering if trauma and this book apply to you. You may be wondering because you may have been traumatized in a way in which there are no visible signs of trauma—for example, no broken bones, no loss of housing.
- In many cases of trauma there are no visible signs. But this does not mean you were not affected.
- The hurt is to your psyche, to your internal self. This invisible part of you is as vulnerable to hurt as your physical body—sometimes more.

- ❧ Think of the human psyche as a jigsaw puzzle made up of many pieces:
  - It takes many years to put it together.
  - It is the result of parenting, education, and interaction with others.
  - Through growing and developing, the psyche becomes whole, at one with itself.
  - We usually don't even notice the psyche until a trauma scatters the pieces. The border may remain intact, but the pieces are in disarray.

- ❧ **You hurt because your insides are in pieces. Your psyche has been shattered.**

Traumatic Reactions Occur in Normal People

- ❧ Some people are afraid of a label like "traumatized."
- ❧ Some people worry it means there is something the matter with them, that they are crazy. But it does *not* mean there is something wrong or abnormal about you.
- ❧ **You are normal . . . what happened to you is not.** What happened to you is out of the range of ordinary human experience. It makes you feel abnormal, different than usual, traumatized, weird. But this is not the same as crazy.
- ❧ Therefore, you need not be afraid to identify yourself as someone who has been traumatized. In fact, giving a name to what ails you can be the first step to recovery. It's like receiving a diagnosis from your medical doctor. Once you have the diagnosis, a treatment plan can be made. If you determine that you have been traumatized, you can then seek help. This book is one example of the help you can find.

PART TWO

Coming Apart in the Immediate Aftermath

---

*A bumper sticker frequently seen in Florida:
"I survived Hurricane Andrew,
but the rebuilding is killing me."*[1]

CHAPTER THREE

The Effect on Your Body and Mind

What has happened to you?

- You have been **shocked.**
- **You are in shock.**
- You are in shock because every aspect of your system went into overload in order to deal with the trauma.
- This is a natural response when trauma hits.
- In fact, it is a protective response. It saves you from having to handle more than you can at one time.
- It also has certain effects that leave you feeling strange.

The Effects of Shock

- You are like a jigsaw puzzle—you have many parts that have come together to make you a whole person.
- When you are shocked, the parts of the puzzle that make you who you are have been disturbed.
- The puzzle that is you has two main categories:
  - Your body.
  - Your mind.
- Shock affects your body and mind in the immediate aftermath. It will leave you . . .

- Physically numb.
- Emotionally numb.
- Perceptually confused.
- Thinking unusually.
- Remembering unclearly.
- Dreaming differently.

Your Body

If you have been **physically injured,** then your body has been shocked by the injury you have sustained.

- Physical injury complicates the trauma; it forces you to deal with a double trauma.
- Physical injury must always receive attention first. In fact, even though you are experiencing psychological trauma, it may go unnoticed until your physical condition has stabilized.
- If your injury was severe, you may be facing a long and arduous recovery and/or permanent disability.
- In these instances, much of the time during the immediate aftermath (and later) will be devoted to attending to your physical needs.

Sometimes shock can block out the existence and source of physical injury. That's what happened to Andrea who was in the January 17, 1994, Southern California earthquake. It wasn't until days later that she really noticed the bump on her head, the dizziness, and the loss of balance. She was still mystified about what had happened until she was looking at insurance photos of the damage. On her bed was her large antique mirror, which had shaken off the wall and which must have hit her on her head. She saw her doctor who confirmed she had a mild concussion and inner ear damage from the blow.[1]

Your Nervous System Reacts

- Sudden and shocking trauma affects your **nervous system.**
    - This is one of the inside hurts that can't be seen. It is experienced by almost everyone, even when there is not external bodily injury.
    - This effect on your nervous system is called different names by those who have studied trauma. The name used here is **hyperarousal.**
    - Hyperarousal occurs because, when the trauma hit, you went on full alert.
    - The odd thing that happens is when the trauma is over you **stay** on full alert.
    - The switch that was turned on doesn't turn off, maintaining the state of hyperarousal.

Hyperarousal

- The **effects of hyperarousal** are:
    - Trouble sleeping.
    - Difficulty concentrating.
    - Heightened vigilance.
    - Being easily startled.
    - Being wary.
    - Sudden crying.
    - Becoming suddenly angry.
    - Being more emotional.
    - Panicking.
    - Intensified alertness.
    - Reminders of the trauma leading to physical reactions—rapid heart beat, sweating, etc.
    - Increased anxiety.

SLEEP DISTURBANCES

Hyperarousal causes **sleep disturbances,** which can take many forms.
- You may take longer to fall asleep.
- You may not be able to fall asleep.
- You may be more sensitive to noise.
- You may awaken more often during the night.
- You may have dreams and/or nightmares about the trauma.
- Repetitive trauma dreams may awaken you and leave you frightened and exhausted.

"I did have dreams after the accident. They only lasted about 30 days and then I didn't have them anymore."[2]
> Mike, after an auto accident

"I thought everything was behind me, but just last week I had severe nightmares, my heart was beating like I was running a marathon. I woke up screaming and yelling for help. I just thought I was going to die and that was the end of it."[3]
> Debra Smathers, after an armed robbery

HEIGHTENED SENSITIVITY

- Another effect from hyperarousal may be an inability to block out repetitive stimuli. For instance, if there is noise from construction nearby, you may find you are unable to block out the sound.
- When you have been traumatized, sometimes you have more trouble managing strong reactions and anxiety.
- Again, it's as if your nervous system is so raw that everything that touches it brings a strong reaction.
- Remember, this is normal and will probably diminish over time.
- Depending on the degree and type of trauma, it may not disappear, but it should get better.

> *"People go about their business. But for almost everyone that lived through one of the biggest earthquakes in California [San Francisco, 1989], life remains different a year after. The differences can be subtle. People may jump when a truck rolls by or when washing machines spin and shake the house. Many people need more time to gain their composure when a small temblor rumbles through. Some people still won't cross the Bay Bridge. Some people have moved away."*[4]

OTHER BODILY REACTIONS

- It is not uncommon to experience physical illness and complaints after trauma.
- These can include:
  - Digestive complaints, ranging from stomachaches to heartburn.
  - Headaches, ranging from mild discomfort to migraines.
  - Allergy symptoms.

> *Many people told me their allergy symptoms worsened following the traumatic event. I spoke with a specialist in this area, Dr. Bernard Geller. He immediately confirmed this phenomenon. Evidently, the stress from the trauma depresses the body's protective ability by interrupting the natural production of cortisone, all of which can lead to an eruption of allergies.*[5]

- A tendency to have colds and viruses and bacterial infections because the stress from the trauma has affected the immune system.
- For women, a change in their normal menstrual cycle, ranging from an interruption to more frequent periods.

> *Many women who experienced the Southern California Northridge earthquake on January 17, 1994, reported various gynecological complaints. One woman, enjoying her play on words, told me she was jolted right out of menopause.*[6]

Your Mind

- Your psyche is made up of many puzzle pieces . . . each is affected by shock and trauma.
- These puzzle pieces are:
  - Your emotions.
  - Your thinking.
  - Your perceptions.
  - Your memory.
  - Your mind in sleep—that is, your dreaming mind.

THE INITIAL IMPACT ON YOUR EMOTIONS: SHOCK

- **Shock** has already been mentioned. It is the first reaction and, in fact, affects every puzzle piece of your mind. For instance:
  - Your emotions are numbed by shock.
  - Your thoughts are of shocked disbelief, leaving you not understanding what you are thinking.
  - Your perceptions are questioned; for example, "I couldn't have seen that correctly!"
  - Your memory seems to be playing tricks on you and you imagine you remembered it wrong and that, perhaps, it wasn't as horrible as you recall.
- Shock and its effects are interwoven throughout the immediate aftermath.

The Initial Impact on Your Emotions: Denial

- **Denial** is another reaction.
- Denial is a way of not acknowledging something that exists.
- It comes in handy when you are unable to cope with the strength of certain emotions in times of great distress, such as when trauma hits.
- Some denial is essential to healing and recovery.
- Denial helps with feelings of . . .
  - Terror.
  - Helplessness.
  - Fear of abandonment.
  - Terror of being hurt again.
  - Fear of dying.
- These feelings would be much too intense without the help of denial. If you were fully aware of your helplessness all at once, you might feel overwhelmed and become incapacitated. Denial allows you to experience only as much of the feeling as you can manage at one time.
- At the early stage after a trauma, denial is a friend and not an enemy.

The Initial Impact on Your Emotions: Other Emotions

- Shock and denial are the main emotional companions during this early phase.
- Other emotions are . . .
  - Confusion and disorientation.
  - Complete calm and numbness.
  - Panic.
  - Weeping.
  - Extreme anxiety.
  - Inflexibility.
  - Insecurity.
  - A feeling of not being in your body, of unrealness.

THE INITIAL IMPACT ON YOUR THINKING: DISBELIEF

- **Disbelief** is, by far, the overriding effect on your thinking.
- At first, you cannot make your thoughts believe what has happened to you.
- Like denial, disbelief is protective.
- It keeps you from believing your thoughts which are, at the moment, incomprehensible.
    - There is no preparation for shocking, sudden events.
    - So, because you couldn't think about this event ahead of time, there is no place in your thoughts for it.
    - A place has to be created in your thoughts *after* the trauma. This is true even for people in hurricanes, when they "know" they are coming—they still cannot believe it happened to *them*.

THE INITIAL IMPACT ON YOUR THINKING: DISORIENTATION AND CONFUSION

- **Disorientation** and **confusion** are two other ways your thoughts are impacted.
    - You will find yourself feeling dizzied by the trauma, which can leave you feeling disoriented. For example, people report becoming easily lost, even in places that have been familiar to them for years.
    - Disorientation and confusion can result in your needing to take more time to accomplish tasks than before. You may be going slower and have to double-think everything you do. It is helpful to allow extra time during this stage.

- It is important to be extra careful. Disorientation can cause incorrect judgments about which actions may or may not be safe. For instance, people are much more accident-prone following a trauma.
- Also, because you are more likely to be confused, you may not be able to make good judgments about important decisions. Just as it is important to slow down actions you may be taking, it is also important to delay decisions.

Robert Bruce was a victim of the Oakland fires in Northern California. He gave advice to the 1993 victims of the Southern California fires. "Take your time," said Bruce. "Just don't hurry . . . spend time with family and friends. Allow the shock to pass before making any decisions." He adds, later, "I think the wisest thing is not to rebuild immediately—to sit down and wait, and collect your wits . . ."[7]

THE INITIAL IMPACT ON YOUR THINKING: UNWANTED THOUGHTS

- There may be unwanted thoughts, unthinkable thoughts, unbelievable thoughts, thoughts like you have never had before.
- These may leave you wondering about yourself—for example, what kind of a person are you, really?
- These sorts of thoughts are predictable given the trauma:
  - You are under enormous pressure and strain as a result of the trauma.
  - This kind of pressure can lead to what psychologists refer to as more primitive ways of thinking.
- Often these unwanted thoughts are angry, hostile ones, like wanting bloody revenge on the person who hurt you!
- Or they may be escapist thoughts in which you want to run away and avoid your responsibilities.

Sally was in Hurricane Iniki on the island of Kauai. She was in the hospital, ready to give birth to a little boy. The hospital was spared, but Sally's home was not. Therefore, when Sally and her husband and newborn left the hospital they had no "home." They had lost everything but each other.

She felt overwhelmed with trying to care for a newborn while in temporary housing. Sally just wanted to go away. She wanted to escape. She understood her wish to escape, but she could not accept the other thoughts she was having. In fact, she was horrified at those thoughts. She wanted to give her baby away. She thought her baby would be better off in another family, with a mother who wasn't so stressed and over-whelmed. Even though these thoughts were motivated by good intentions and worry that she wasn't able to give the baby what the baby needed, she thought her thoughts were "terrible." She had trouble being compassionate with herself. Her thoughts seemed unforgivable. But, really, they were just thoughts—nothing more than an expression of Sally's stress and strain and exhaustion and dislocation.[8]

THE INITIAL IMPACT ON YOUR PERCEPTIONS

- If this is the first time you've experienced a trauma, you may be seeing the world differently from before.
- This may not happen immediately, but over time, as your denial and disbelief lessen, the world may seem different.
  - The world may not feel safe.
  - The world may not feel steady.
  - The world may not feel predictable.
  - The world may not feel fair.
- And because the world isn't the way you thought it was, you may be questioning the way you perceived it. How is it really? Is it the old way or the new?
- It may be most helpful just to let yourself know that these questions are normal and that eventually they will be answered.
- Sometimes, however, there is a tendency to fight allowing a new perception to take form. The wish is for everything to be the way it was and it can't be if you have to fit in this new puzzle piece.
- The **most challenging task of this early stage** is to just live with the confusion, to live with the pieces being in disarray and not try to put them back into place before they are ready to fit. Let time have its way.

Judie ended up questioning just about everything because of the freak auto accident that literally turned her upside down. She agreed to speak with me about it at my home one bright sunny morning. Her smile and her style matched the morning. She was striking in both appearance and manner, and my first impression didn't hint at the fragility that became apparent when she spoke about what happened to her.

Before Judie told me about her trauma, she said she lived her life in a safe, protective bubble. Almost nothing bad had happened to her. She had never been in a hospital, her family had been healthy, she had pursued and found just about everything she wanted from her life. The only glitch she could think of was the time she bit her tongue and had to have stitches.

For almost four decades, Judie's world had been friendly, fair, and reliable. Her world was not a place where you would be driving along, enjoying a conversation with a fellow worker about a successful sales call, and suddenly have a mangled metal ladder in the road in front of you. Her world was not a place where you would have to swerve to miss the ladder and suddenly fishtail across the freeway on-ramp, and by some miracle not hit anything. And her world was not a place where, after avoiding collision, the car goes off the ramp, down a hill, flips on its side and then over on its roof, and then inexplicably turns over one last time, landing upright on the ramp below, in the opposite direction of traffic. This was not Judie's world. This was some new world. This was a world that was unfair, unpredictable, and unsafe.

Because of the accident, Judie's view of the world changed dramatically. She made two changes immediately. She was raised to hang in there and see things through, but the accident caused her to question that belief. She walked away from her job soon after the accident because she realized life was too short to do something she didn't like. She made that change and felt good about it. With a tone of wryness, she then told me about the second change that was not as dramatic, but significant—she bought a Volvo (commonly believed to be one of the safest cars on the road).

Her next step was to conquer her fear of driving. The fear was almost uncontrollable. She was terrified and sure she would have another accident. Her way of dealing with her terror was to change her "self-talk." For Judie, this meant noticing when she was having "terrifying" thoughts about driving and altering those thoughts. She did this by reminding herself she was in control and that she was doing the best she could. Judie said all of this helped and she can now drive, even though she never enters her car without worrying how the trip will be.

After quitting her job, buying the Volvo, and conquering her fear of driving, Judie began wrestling with the internal changes set in motion by the trauma. Her accident had jarred and permanently changed her view of the world. The puzzle pieces of her life were thrown into disarray, and she had to put them back into place in a new way in order to reconcile her shocking experience. Her new world view had to include the fact that someone can be fine one moment and not fine the next. As a result, she now wonders what might happen when she drives, when her husband goes to work, or when they go out on a weekend morning for a cup of coffee. Judie didn't worry about these things before, but she does now because she knows that unexpected, startling, and life-threatening occurrences can happen to anyone.

She finds herself living much more in the moment. Living in the moment has resulted in her being more in charge of her life. She no longer lets things go until the next day because she knows there may not be a next day. Every day she asks herself if she has done what she needed to do and if she has said what she needed to say.

It has been many years since her bizarre mis-hap, and Judie is still amazed how one event could have made such a difference in her life. But she doesn't doubt that it has. She's also amazed about something else that lingers from the accident: it is the sound of the crunch—that crunch from when the roof caved in from the car spiraling down the hill. Remembering that crunch reminds her that a split second can change everything. The sound doesn't constantly haunt her, but it does occasionally reverberate, and when it does she remembers to be thankful she is alive.

She is also thankful for one other fact—even though her bubble burst, she still felt surrounded by something protective. After she landed on that ramp below, she amazingly had only a pin-prick of blood on her left forefinger where a tiny piece of glass had pierced her skin. She didn't even need a Band-Aid.[9]

OTHER IMPACTS ON YOUR PERCEPTIONS

- There is another way in which your perceptions can be affected.
- This is by actually not being able to believe what you see.
- This most often happens in natural disasters, when nature has turned what you knew upside down.

Dorothy talked about trying to make sense from nonsense. She and her family were in Hurricane Andrew. They spent the night in the home of a friend who was a builder. He had built a hurricane-proof home, so Dorothy and her family felt relatively safe during the hurricane. The morning after the storm, she and her husband left for home on foot. The walk between her home and their friend's home usually took thirty minutes. This time it took two and a half hours.

It was over 100 degrees and maximum humidity. They walked among ruins, hoping they were walking in the right direction. They couldn't know for sure their direction was correct because no landmarks remained. Everything was flattened, damaged, or just plain gone.

Dorothy was able to describe in minute detail how the hurricane had left things looking. She is a keen observer. Perhaps this skill is what made it so difficult for her to believe what she saw. She knew, without a doubt, every detail of the way things had looked before the storm. So when she stood in front of her townhouse complex, exhausted from the heat and the strain, she couldn't believe her eyes. All of the houses looked as if they were out of place, as if they had been moved around. They appeared this way because pieces of them were missing and the trees that had been standing in front of them had been knocked down. She questioned herself, telling herself she knew what the neighborhood had looked like before, so how could she not remember now? She wondered how this could now not be a row of houses when yesterday it was. It was a visual mystery beyond anything she could imagine.

Her husband had begun to noticeably tire about halfway through their walk home. Dorothy kept encouraging him, sometimes almost dragging him along. At the point when they arrived at the entrance to their complex, he asked her how much farther they had to go. She was stunned. He did not know he was standing in front of the home where he had lived for fifteen years, nor did he know he was standing in the driveway that he had driven in and out of a thousand times. She told him they *were home, but he couldn't see it. She pulled him out onto the street, directing him to look at an area where more structures remained intact. He still couldn't see it. It was like a photograph had been cut into minute pieces and his eye and mind couldn't put them back together again.*[10]

THE INITIAL IMPACT ON YOUR MEMORY: TRAUMATIC MEMORY

- The memory of traumatic events is unlike any other type of memory.
- **Traumatic memory** is like an engraving on the brain. It is a clear, distinct, vivid image.
- Traumatic memory seems to stand by itself. It's like the difference between a still shot and a movie.
- But, it is a still shot in vibrant, living color and is filled with emotional intensity. It is a memory that has impact.

Remember Judie's comment: "You know, you never forget what it sounds like, that crunch."[11]

THE INITIAL IMPACT ON YOUR MEMORY: FORGETFULNESS

- Another aspect of memory that you may notice in the immediate aftermath is that you may find yourself being **forgetful.**
- You may find your **short-term memory has been affected.**
- This can be frustrating, confusing, and worrisome. It is usually not something that lasts.
- It is helpful to:
    - Make notes to remind yourself of appointments, phone numbers, or addresses.
    - Make those around you aware of your forgetfulness and ask to be reminded.
    - Reduce your expectations of yourself by not expecting yourself to remember the way you did before the trauma.

> *Mary was in the path of Hurricane Andrew. Afterward, she worried a great deal about her forgetfulness and shortened attention span because she was afraid it distracted her from parenting. Her husband also suffered from forgetfulness in those first six months after Andrew. They would attempt to recall information they had known before, something simple like a familiar phone number, but it just wasn't there.*[12]

THE INITIAL IMPACT ON YOUR DREAMS

- Your dreams may be exact replicas of the trauma.
- But, then, again, they may not. **Traumatic dreams** can take many different forms. In fact, sometimes they are so disguised you don't even realize they are directly related to the trauma.

- But whatever form they take, they can be disturbing.
  - They are disturbing because they don't let you escape from the trauma.
  - They are disturbing because they wake you up.
  - They are disturbing because they leave you feeling out of control. It's another reminder the trauma owns you for a while instead of you owning the trauma.
- Unfortunately, trauma dreams are often a fact of the post-trauma time. That is, they are normal given what you have gone through.
- It is helpful to keep in mind that dreams are a part of your effort to come to terms with the trauma.

The Inevitable Review

- There is another phenomenon that sometimes occurs soon after the trauma.
- It is a review of what you did before and during the trauma.
- It is an attempt to gain control by thinking about what you could or should have done.
- The purpose is to try to make sense of the question, "Why did this happen?"
- Many people think they should have behaved differently, both before and during the trauma. This is the **"I could have, I should have, I would have"** response.
- It may be you could have behaved in a more preventive way before the trauma in order to escape or reduce the impact of the trauma. For instance, if you live in earthquake or hurricane or tornado country, there are certain precautions that can minimize the chance of injury.
- **But usually it isn't true that you could have behaved differently during the trauma.**
- Something takes over during a trauma and you just react the way you react.
- No one really knows how he or she is going to react during a trauma. What you think you might do and what you actually do are often two completely different things.

> *Andrea was stunned when she realized she had torn a door from its hinges in order to reach her animals during the earthquake. She never would have thought she had that strength.*[13]

ੈ Your actions during a trauma are not dictated by your thoughts. Usually there isn't time for the luxury of thought—you just react.

ੈ What is most important is **you survived**. Whatever you did, you survived—nothing else really matters.

> *Jim was very clear about the fact that what you end up doing when a trauma hits is very different from what you think you will do. This tall and slender gray-haired banker in his fifties rides bikes. It is his passion; it is his danger. He has the fortune, and perhaps the misfortune, of living on one of the most beautiful and treacherous highways in the world, the one with which every Southern Californian has a love-hate relationship—the Pacific Coast Highway, locally known as PCH.*
>
> *Jim was relishing the "good ride" he was about to finish. He was traveling at twenty-five to thirty miles per hour when a car turned left in front of him. There was no decision to make. None. There was only the crash. "It's the sort of thing that happened so quickly. You don't have time. You always think, well, I'm a good rider, I'll be able to avoid anything, it's not going to be a problem. Well, in reality, it happened so fast, you don't [have time]. It was so quick. It surprised me. I slammed right into the side of the car. Everything went black at that point."*

Jim did say that just before the crash there was time for one split-second thought. Playfully, he asked me to guess what it was. I sat blank for a moment and then it hit me. "Oh, shit!" I said. He laughed heartily at my guessing correctly.

Jim didn't actually suffer from the "I could have, I would have, I should have" response. He's pretty much in touch with the reality of these things and knows there was nothing he could have or should have done, and that he didn't have any choice about the would have. This saved Jim from having much psychological trauma from this incident. He did, however, suffer otherwise. Both of his hands were crushed, one more than the other. He had three surgeries, one which left thirty-nine pins in one hand for some time. He also needed a new thumb knuckle, so a man-made one was constructed to replace the one that was crushed. And because he could not use either hand, he had a prolonged period of helplessness. This was, in many ways, the most difficult. He jokes about it, but it was clear he was not happy about having to be fed and dressed and driven to and from work. But his unhappiness with his forced state of helplessness did not interfere with his expressing the gratitude he felt for the help he had during that long year of recovery.

After that year, this man who loves bicycling was careful when he pedaled down the Pacific Coast Highway. He went slow. He checked cars. He did both for a while. Now, however, even though he is generally more careful, he no longer goes slow. He knows that if something happened, there wouldn't be much he could do anyway, so he may as well go fast and feel the Southern California wind in his face.[14]

CHAPTER FOUR

What Helps

Everyone Is Different

- The previous chapter talked about the effects of trauma on the body and mind during the immediate aftermath. The immediate aftermath may last an hour, a day, a week, or even months.
- The immediate aftereffects and the length of time they last vary across people because . . .
  - Everyone is different.
  - Effects don't happen in a step-wise progression.
  - Every trauma is different.
- However, what is true for everyone is that there is an initial shake-up. The puzzle pieces have been disturbed.
- It is also true that there are some basic steps to follow in the immediate aftermath in order to take care of yourself.

Basic Steps for Action

- The **basic steps** for action are:
  - If you were physically injured, you must acquire the necessary medical attention, if you haven't already done so.
  - You must **establish a sense of safety.** Depending on the nature of the trauma, this will take different forms. **You and *only* you** can decide about what will bring you a sense of safety. Other people may think they know what works for you, or may think

what you want to do is silly, but **they are not you.**
They haven't had your experience and, therefore,
cannot possibly know what will make you feel safe.
For example:

- After a natural disaster, safety might come in the
  form of first finding shelter and second repairing
  your home (if it was damaged).
- After a criminal assault, establishing safety might
  mean securing your home with improved locks
  and lighting, starting to carry mace, or taking a
  self-defense class.
- After an auto accident, you may wish to purchase
  a safer car.

*Two victims of the Northridge, California,
earthquake in January 1994 said:*

*"I slept in my clothes. I didn't want to take
showers—it made me feel too vulnerable to take
my clothes off."* [1]

*"I carried a flashlight in my pants waistband
and kept one between my pillows—it wasn't
good enough to have it on my nightstand."* [2]

PHYSICAL ROUTINES

- **Physical routines** are very important. Routines include:
  - Trying to reestablish regular sleeping habits.
  - Maintaining regular eating habits.
  - Trying to resist the temptation of numbing sub-
    stances—for example, alcohol or drugs.
  - Returning to your exercise regimen or establishing
    one if you didn't have one before the trauma.
- Physical routines are important:
  - They will help you feel you are in control of your
    life by providing structure, safety, and regularity.

Establishing control is the first big step toward recovery.

- You need rest and caretaking. Going through a trauma is extremely discombobulating. Even though you may not have been physically hurt, you need as much TLC as if you were.

SOME EXTRA HELP

- What if you try to reestablish your physical routines and you cannot? What if the trauma won't let you?
- What if, for instance, your attempts at healing are constantly thwarted by sleep disturbances?
- This may be the time to call in extra help.
- Many people hate this next suggestion because it makes them feel more out of control. But, if you can't sleep you will have no chance for recovery.
- The extra help is **medication** that is prescribed by a doctor.
- If you are freaked out at this suggestion, it is understandable. However, if you can think of it as a decision to put yourself back in control, it can be extremely helpful.
- And, most important, it is **temporary**. It is only to help you get through this tough time, when it is so essential to have regular routines. And, it will speed up recovery.
- A psychiatrist who understands trauma's effects is the type of doctor to seek out. The reason for this is that there are specific drugs for helping with intrusive memories and trauma-related sleep disturbances.
- Try not to let yourself get to the point of being sleep-deprived before you take this action. Lack of sleep will be too hard on your psyche and on your physical self, and will prevent you from healing more quickly.

DEFINING YOUR NEEDS

- Another aspect of taking care of yourself has to do with defining your needs.
- Everyone is different. Therefore, your needs will be different. For example,
  - Some people find it really helpful to stay active.
  - Some people find it recuperative to be quiet.
  - Some people feel better being alone.
  - Some people like being with others some of the time and alone some of the time.
  - Some people have a need to talk repeatedly about the trauma. You may need to talk more than one person can listen to you. If so, find several outlets for your thoughts: for example, talking to several different people, hotlines, journal writing.
- There is *no right way* to do it. The only way is **your** way.
- Your way may be one way one moment, and another way the next.
- Give yourself room to define your needs from moment to moment.

LIMITED CHOICES

- It is very likely, in the beginning, that your choices will be limited.
- For instance, even though you may want to work at the same level you were working before the trauma, you just may not be able.
- The trauma may dictate what you can and cannot do.
- This can be infuriating and frustrating, because it means the trauma is still in charge. It is a hard fact to face, but a fact it is.
- However, there is a paradox here, because the quickest way to feel in charge is to accept the fact you are not in control. The essence of feeling and being in control is not needing control.

> *Jim, the bicycle rider, hated the fact that he had to have help in the bathroom. Who wouldn't? But as he said, he had no choice, so he took the help for what it was worth (which happened to be a lot).*[3]

Getting Help

YOUR INITIAL RESPONSE TO HELP

- Thinking you need help and getting help are both difficult for most people.
- It leaves people feeling more helpless and out of control to think of themselves as someone who needs help.
- But imagine what you would do if you were physically injured (and maybe you were during the trauma). You wouldn't think twice about getting help. You would just do it.
- So, consider just doing it in this case, as well.

What Sort of Help Do You Need in the Beginning?

- The help you need in the beginning is a different sort from what you might need later on.
- First, you need help that will get you back into your normal routines.
- As mentioned, that could mean **medication,** but maybe not. You may only need to let those around you and let yourself know that routine is essential, and then put it into place.
- The other thing that will help is **information.** Information is very grounding. It will help you understand what is happening to you and help you feel in control.
- This book provides all the basic information you need.
- You may recall the earlier discussion about how hard it is to process information.
- Because of that, you may need to have the information repeated or you may need to reread this early chapter often.
- Also, some of us understand better through our ears than through our eyes, so it may be helpful for someone to read this to you.
- See the next page. It sums up everything about the immediate aftermath in a quick review list for you to reread when you need it.

Quick Review List for the Immediate Aftermath

- You have been traumatized.
- You are probably having some unusual thoughts, feelings, perceptions, and dreams.
- This does not mean you are abnormal. It means only that you've gone through an abnormal experience.
- You have probably experienced **shock.**
- Shock is a protective reaction and is normal.
- Both your body and your mind have been shocked.
- You may have suffered physical injury that requires medical attention.
- You have also suffered a shock to your nervous system.
- This has left you in a state called **hyperarousal.**
- Hyperarousal leads to difficulty sleeping, being easily startled, being very anxious, being very watchful, panicking easily, and having difficulty concentrating.
- You may need **medication** to deal with hyperarousal.
- You may also be in a state of **denial.** This is normal at this stage, as it helps you deal with overwhelming and unmanageable feelings—for example, terror.
- You may be in a state of **disbelief.** This is normal and protective.
- **Making yourself safe** will help.
- **Getting into routines** will help.
- **Doing what is right for you** will help.
- Accepting that the trauma has control over you is the first step to achieving control over the trauma.

PART THREE

The Middle Period of Disarray

Be patient toward all that is unsolved in your heart and try to love the questions themselves . . . Do not . . . seek the answers, which cannot be given you because you would not be able to live them. And the point is to live everything. Live the questions now. Perhaps you will . . . gradually, without noticing it, live along some distant day into the answer.[1]

CHAPTER FIVE

Preliminary Thoughts

- The reactions that immediately follow trauma have been reviewed. Now, what happens next?
- The middle phase comes next, but it may be mixed with aspects from the immediate aftermath and from the resolution phase. This is because:
  - The phases of recovery aren't very orderly.
  - In some ways, recovery parallels trauma itself. Trauma and recovery are, by their nature, chaotic.
- There is no specific time period for any phase.
  - For some, the immediate aftermath may be an hour. For others, it could be weeks.
  - The middle period may begin quickly and continue for various lengths of time, from weeks to months to years.
  - How long each phase lasts depends on the individual and the trauma.
- However, there is one thing about time as it relates to the phases of recovery: **The middle phase is almost always the longest and, therefore, the most difficult to get through.**
- Several areas are stressed in this section on the middle phase. They are:
  - Your physical self.
  - Your emotions.
  - Your thoughts and perceptions.
  - Others' reactions to you and you to them.

A Quick Reminder

- If you were physically injured and it was serious, you may be focusing almost entirely on the work of rehabilitating. You may be spending most of your time concentrating on physical therapy or other aspects of physical recovery. Therefore, the middle phase of psychological recovery may be delayed or different from those who were not physically injured.

- Because this book is mostly about the emotional aftermath of trauma, you may want to do other reading if you were seriously or permanently injured from the trauma (see Appendix A).

- Even if you were not physically injured, you may continue to have physical hyperarousal reactions such as sleep disturbances, heightened vigilance, and so on. You may want to review the pages in Chapter 3 on hyperarousal because it may linger.

- Physical routines are important, no matter which phase of recovery you are going through.

CHAPTER SIX

Denial and Intrusions

- Of all the psychological and emotional responses, there are two that are particularly striking and specific only to trauma:
    - Denial.
    - Intrusions.
- **DENIAL** is a way of not acknowledging that something exists. It's an ingenious psychological mechanism because it can be very helpful in times of great stress.
- **INTRUSIONS** are a flood—a flood of memories, a flood of images, a flood of knowing. And like a flood, they overwhelm and seem to have the potential to destroy.
- Denial and intrusions are two separate experiences that interact. This is the way they'll be looked at here, both as separate and as interacting.
- Denial and intrusions can be mild to extreme. Not everyone who goes through trauma necessarily experiences these phenomena.

Denial

- **Denial** is a way of acting as if something doesn't exist. This may make it sound like you wake up the morning after your trauma and say to yourself, "Self, today you are going to deny _____."
- This is not the way it works.
- Denial is unconscious. It is exactly like all of the other defenses humans use. That is, until we are aware of our defenses, they remain in our unconscious.

- Defenses, in general—and denial, in particular—have sometimes received a bad rap.
- Defenses—and specifically, denial—are not necessarily bad or pathological. As a matter of fact, they are necessary for optimal human functioning as they protect us from being overwhelmed.
- Denial following trauma is usually essential to help you get through this overwhelming event.

FORMS OF DENIAL

- Denial can take many forms.
  - You believe you are all right. You may return to work, go through your daily routine, all the while ignoring the gravity of what you went through, perhaps even making light of it.
  - You may feel a sense of strangeness in the world, like a feeling of not really being there. This is the result of having to block out part of the reality.
  - You may look at the trauma and think it wasn't too bad, given what you went through and what could have happened.

> *Mary was in Hurricane Andrew. She had remarkable odds to cope with—the loss of her home, living with relatives for weeks, caring for a toddler and a newborn, and yet she said to me, "I knew there were people that were worse off than me."*[1]

- You may deny it happened at all or acknowledge that it happened but think it was milder than it actually was.
- Denial may show up in actions. You put yourself in the same situation in which the trauma occurred—for example, going out alone at night in an unsafe area.
- Whatever form it takes, denial can be both protective and worrisome.

DENIAL AS PROTECTIVE

~ How does denial protect you?
  - It protects you from the full impact of the trauma.
  - It protects you from feeling the fear or, in extreme traumas, the terror that accompanied what happened to you.
  - It protects you from feeling the fear and terror about it happening again.
  - It buys you time. In a way, it's like going to sleep. Sleep, in times of trauma and other distresses, can be very healing. Denial, because it functions like sleep, can be healing as well. It gives your system a break.

Many years have passed since the incident that led Nancy Becker-Kennedy to spend her life in a wheelchair. Now almost forty, she was twenty the day she went swimming in a lake at the home of friends. Nancy watched her friend dive off the end of the pier into the lake. Then she dove, not realizing the lake was too shallow for the angle of her dive. Her head hit the bottom, snapping her neck back. Instantly, Nancy realized her limbs were useless. Helplessly, she swirled under the water while thinking no one on the pier or shore was aware of what was happening. As the seconds passed, she'd surrendered to the idea of death, and with the surrender came a sense of calm. The calm was a surprise because, for as long as she could remember, she had battled with a terror of death. But here she was, facing death, and there was no terror. Her thoughts focused on her life. Her only regret was she had not had a boyfriend whom she really loved.

In the moment before completely letting go, Nancy was pulled out of the water. The ambulance arrived and the paramedics immobilized her with sandbags to reduce the chance of further injury. As Nancy was being put into the ambulance, she realized she was paralyzed and then she "forgot." She had entered a state of extreme denial. The reality of being paralyzed was unbearable.

Years later, Nancy wrote a screenplay entitled Always a Woman. It is about the months following the accident. She called this her period of post-traumatic psychosis. The main character is named Dinah (Nancy). The story is about Dinah's battle with the denial of her paralysis and how she fought off the reality of being in a wheelchair, and as a result, went bonkers for a while. Psychically, she had no choice. She needed the safety of denial, a state many would call crazy because they wouldn't understand that it was sane for her to go crazy in order to protect her sanity. If she had been forced to face the reality of her loss all at once and too early, then she may not have been able to recover.

At that time, the traditional medical approach called for confronting the patient about denial. Fortunately, Dinah/Nancy's doctor understood the trauma was also to her psyche and vehemently disagreed with the other medical staff about confronting her. This protected Dinah/Nancy from experiencing too much reality too soon. His intervention and protection of Dinah allowed her to leave reality when she needed to and to face reality when she could. Without this . . . well, it's hard to say, but it was obvious her psyche called upon this protective device to save her from something even more alarming than knowing she was paralyzed.

The screenplay shows Dinah fighting reality by trying to sell her pre-accident boyfriend on her omnipotence in order to convince him not to leave her: "Oh, Stan . . . I moved my toe yesterday, they say that's the first thing to come back. Stan, just keep an open mind. You know if I did anything wrong, I can change it. You know me, I can change anything."

And then in the screenplay Dinah tells us her wish: to have her legs feel warm. Having the wish reveals that she knew she was paralyzed without letting herself know that she knew. She hallucinated a nonparalyzed state as she told an attendant, "See, if I was just red, I'd know I was warm. Warm like God's hot ocean . . . because I'm red and warm as God's hot ocean. I'm just floating so gentle."

The belief that she could change anything and the hallucinated state of redness and warmth helped her continue to deny the permanency of her state and the massiveness of her loss.

Over time, and little by little, she came to know what she knew all along. She knew just as soon as she could, not sooner or later. Gradually she became fully conscious of her circumstances and finally accepted her chair. Over time, the chair became a mere backdrop for this beautiful woman who now spends her life as a professional comedienne and as an activist for the disabled. She is a classic example of someone who went insane to stay sane. Nancy's experience instructs us about the alternating process of denial and intrusive knowing, and helps us know that if we give time to this process, reality and life will prevail.[2]

NONPROTECTIVE DENIAL

❧   Denial is **not** protective . . .
- When it puts you in situations of danger.
  - For example, if you were carjacked yet thereafter did not take the usual precautions of locking your car doors because you believed it could not happen again, then denial is operating in a way that is not protective.
- When you use fantasies to such a degree that you cannot register the parts of reality that will help you protect yourself in the future.
  - For example, you may fantasize that the next time you would react differently by being more bold or more clever.
  - It is impossible, however, to predict how you will react. Even if you tried to think through every scenario in order to attempt to prepare, it would make little difference because there is no way to know just how the next time will occur. (We would all like to think we can be a John Wayne or an Arnold Schwarzenegger in their best roles, but sadly we are not.)

❧   The best protection is providing for your safety through action, rather than imagining how you will react through fantasy.

Intrusions

- Protective denial guards you from its opposite—**intrusions.**
- Intrusions take the form of . . .
  - Flashbacks.
  - Recurring memories of the trauma.
  - The overwhelming feelings of . . .
    - Terror.
    - Extreme anxiety.
    - Helplessness.
    - Rage.
  - Confusions.
  - Unwanted and frightening dreams.
  - Unexpected and painful bodily sensations.

INTRUSIONS AS FLASHBACKS

- **Flashbacks** are sudden, vivid images of the trauma that seem to come from nowhere.
- Flashbacks make it seem like the event is happening *now.*
- That is, during a flashback, there is no distinction between the trauma being remembered and the present. Flashbacks even include the attendant physical reactions, such as sweating, increased heart rate, and hair standing on end.
- *Flashbacks are a normal reaction* to what has happened to you.
- But flashbacks are also frightening because there is a fear you might, in a sense, become caught in them.
- Remember, flashbacks pass. If you are having flashbacks, it may be helpful to know that they do end, just as the traumatic event ended.
- *You will not stay in the flashbacks for long.*
- If flashbacks persist over time, seek help from a trauma counselor. There are techniques available to help control flashbacks. Take advantage of professional help.

INTRUSIONS AS MEMORIES

- **Memories** of the trauma are different from flashbacks.
- Sometimes memories are not accompanied by feelings. They are isolated from the feelings, not unlike watching a silent slide show.
- However, like flashbacks, intrusive memories can be accompanied by all of the unpleasant feelings of the event. But you are aware that it is a *memory*.
- Because you are involuntarily recalling the event, it is an intrusion. The involuntary nature of the memory makes it unpleasant at best.

> *Actress Kelly McGillis commented during our interview about the way a memory can just overwhelm someone: "I haven't thought about [the rape] in a while. It was a whole lifetime ago. It's funny though, I will tell you something that's very strange. I'm doing this play [1994—twelve years later] and I have this scene where a man threatens my character and one night, in the middle of the performance, it struck some kind of visceral memory where I just started crying; I couldn't stop. For the first time in my life I realized that any traumatic experience we go through is somehow kept and stored, and for some reason that one time or one word triggers a whole chain of emotional responses not felt for years. Right when it happened, I knew what was happening. It was like being on an out-of-control train. You can't stop it."*[3]

INTRUSIONS AS OVERWHELMING FEELINGS

ᴥ Intrusions can be experienced as
  - Terror.
  - Extreme anxiety.
  - Helplessness.
  - Rage.
  - Intense sadness and grief.

ᴥ These and other feelings may accompany a memory of the event.

ᴥ Or they may be experienced, but remain isolated from the memory.

ᴥ In this circumstance, it may seem they come out of nowhere.

ᴥ But with some scrutiny, you will probably discover that *something* triggered them. That something will always be connected to the trauma.

ᴥ It may be something obvious or something remote, but it will always be linked. For example, if you were assaulted by someone, the feelings might be triggered by seeing someone who looked similar to the person who hurt you.

ᴥ Knowing the feelings are linked makes them more manageable. In recognizing the link, you can let yourself know that the intrusion was triggered by something tied to the past and had nothing to do with the present. This way you can begin to differentiate past from present, which begins to make the present safe.

INTRUSIONS AS CONFUSIONS

ᴥ Intrusions can be experienced as **confusions.**
  - Sometimes intrusions confuse you because you suddenly feel you are in the moment when it happened.
  - Sometimes they confuse you because they create strong feelings and you don't know why.

- Intrusions as confusions are **disorienting.** You may suddenly feel you don't know where you are and that you don't know what period of time you are in.
- This can be alarming because it makes you feel as if you are not in charge of yourself.
- Once again, confusions are to be expected and are not unusual. It is one of the ways your unconscious is attempting to deal with what happened to you.

INTRUSIONS AS DREAMS

- Intrusions can be **unwanted and frightening dreams.**
- Just as flashbacks, memories, overwhelming feelings, and confusions can occur during waking hours, they can also occur in dreams.

> *Shawnee had terrifying nightmares where she was chased by "guys with guns." They were nightmares that intruded violently into her sleep, as the two men had intruded violently into her life.*[4]

- Dream images often are just as vivid and repetitive as daytime flashbacks and memories, and they usually include intense feelings.
- If these types of dreams are occurring, you may also be experiencing:
  - An inability to fall asleep.
  - Sleep deprivation.
  - Fear of sleeping.
  - Night terrors.
  - Night sweats.
- If they persist and are too disruptive, you may need to get help to deal with their effects, via counseling or medication.

Shawnee realized she had to do something about the nightmares that were leaving her drained and exhausted. She went for help and they soon ended.[5]

THE UPSIDE OF INTRUSIONS

- It may be hard to believe there is an upside to intrusions, but there is.
- As with most aspects of how our psyche operates, there is more than one side to the story.
- Intrusions are **attempts to confront the trauma.**
- Our minds cannot forget what has not been remembered. In order to really resolve something and make it part of our life experience, it needs to become part of our life story.
- Traumatic experience, until it becomes a part of us, has the potential to be reexperienced in its original form— that is, as a trauma. However, when it becomes a part of you, it is a puzzle piece that fits into and together with the rest of you.
- Each time there is an intrusion, there is an opportunity to deal with the trauma and make it a piece of the puzzle that is you. The intrusion can become an opportunity to think about the trauma in order to understand it and its meaning, to put it in perspective, and to resolve it by putting it into place.
- The goal in this process is to no longer have the trauma be a puzzle piece that is floating off by itself, out of your control. Each intrusion is a chance to capture that piece and make it yours.

The Interplay Between Denial and Intrusions

- If denial and intrusions are part of your reaction to the trauma, you will most likely find yourself alternating between one and the other. This is quite common. You emerge from denial to face the painful and intrusive memory and then retreat to denial again.

- This process can protect you as well as help you. However, if you find yourself going back and forth between denial and intrusions, with no change in intensity, you are in a state of being retraumatized. That is, each time is like going through the trauma over again. There is no value in this.

- The value of intrusions comes from gaining control over them. Control comes from
  - Being able to think about the meaning of the event.
  - Thinking about your perceptions of the event as they relate to how you view yourself.
  - Being able to harness your feelings so that you have control over them instead of their having control over you.

CHAPTER SEVEN

Other Emotional Reactions

- There are other emotional reactions that can be expected.
- These are what I call the **feeling small feelings**. They include feeling a **loss of control, a sense of incompetence, and a sense of helplessness.**
- Then there are the **raw emotional aftereffects.** These feelings are those of:
    - **Terror and/or intense fear.**
    - **Rage and anger.**
    - **Panic.**
    - **Mood swings.**
    - **Extreme anxiety.**
- **Constriction** and **numbing** are two reactions to the raw emotional aftereffects.
- Finally, there may be a feeling of **depression.**

Feeling Small

❧ The **feeling small** feelings are:
- Inadequacy.
- Powerlessness and helplessness.
- Being unable to do what you did before the trauma.
- Physical vulnerability.
- Dependency and, therefore, feeling a loss of autonomy.
- Shame from feeling small in a grown-up body.

❧ You are left with these feelings because the trauma took away your sense of yourself as an adult. The trauma was like an angry, punishing parent, reminding you who the boss really is.

> *"There was such a loss of control when it hit [the January 1994 Southern California quake]. It was arbitrary, malevolent. The earth was angry and betrayed me. I didn't hold it against the house, I held it against the earth."*[1]

❧ Most of us are unprepared for feeling like a child. It will feel like a shock that the grown-up part of you has been ripped away.

❧ It will take time and patience to realign yourself with your adult self and to put the trauma into perspective.

The Raw Emotional Aftereffects: Terror and Fear

- Terror and/or intense fear are usually connected specifically to what occurred. That is, you will be afraid **the trauma will reoccur**—that there will be another hurricane or another mugging.

> *After Judie's car accident, she said the real trauma was the fear of driving again. She was sure she would have another accident if she wasn't very careful, and she had to use what she called "self-talk" to overcome her fear of driving.*[2]

- Terror is also related to **death**. It may be the first time in your life that you came close to death. The trauma has forced you to realize your mortality in a most unkind and graphic way.

- Terror and/or fear may be **triggered** by seemingly unthreatening things. For instance, you may find yourself feeling afraid of the dark or of certain types of roadways or of going out of doors.

- Usually, these feelings take on fearful proportions because they are in some way linked with the trauma and/or with feelings of safety. That is, you may feel safe only in the light of day and only indoors. Or you may feel fearful of a roadway that is like the one you were on at the time of the accident.

- As time passes, the effects of the trauma subside, and these terrors and fears will also subside. *If they do not,* this is an indication that it may be time to seek trauma-related counseling. Resolution of the trauma will bring resolution of intense fears and terror.

The Raw Emotional Aftereffects: Rage and Anger

- **Rage and anger** may seem to erupt without reason.
- They may be directed at anyone or no one.
- They may be directed where you think they shouldn't.
- Rage and anger may frighten you because the feelings:
  - Seem to come from nowhere.
  - Seem to be unfairly directed.
  - Make you feel out of control.
  - Seem like they will never end.
  - Don't seem nice.
- Rage and anger are normal. Of course you're angry about what happened.

Hurricane Andrew disrupted Mary's life, leaving nothing the same. She felt resentful and angry toward a lot of people—toward relatives who seemed caught up in trivia, toward neighbors who didn't have as much disruption and damage, toward the government, contractors, everyone. She said she thought a lot of the anger was displaced, but she couldn't stop herself from being angry. It was difficult for her to realize that her anger made sense. But as I listened to her talk about losing her entire home, and with it everything that was familiar, I thought to myself, "Of course, you are angry. Who in their right mind wouldn't be?"[3]

The Raw Emotional Aftereffects: Panic

- You may also be feeling **panic.** Panic is the experience of coming apart inside. You feel like you are collapsing, leading to the fear you can't cope. Panic is the fear associated with being unable to cope and with the fear you will be harmed or terrorized again.
- The aftereffect of panic can be triggered by a variety of circumstances, such as
  - Being alone, which leaves you feeling small and unprotected as you may have been during the trauma.
  - Being in a place or situation like the trauma, making you fear it will happen again.
  - Remembering how close you came to death.
  - Being overwhelmed by what you are now facing in order to reconstruct your life.
  - Knowing the world is not the safe and predictable place you thought it to be.
  - Sounds, smells, and types of touch that remind you of the event.

The Raw Emotional Aftereffects: Mood Swings

- It is day 92 after the trauma and you suddenly notice you're feeling pretty good—what a relief! You figure the day has finally come that you can say to yourself and others, "It's over. I'm over the effects of this event."
- You feel good on day 93 and day 94. You relax.
- Then, on the morning of day 95, it hits. You wake up from a terror dream and you feel vulnerable all over again. Recognizing your vulnerability, you feel depressed—it's happened again and there was nothing you could do to stop it.
- You feel betrayed by your own psyche. It fooled you into thinking you were through your recovery.

- This is the tough part about mood swings, and this is what makes them so hard to deal with.
- Even though it may feel like it, **you have not slipped all the way back.** These fluctuations are temporary and should be expected. They are part of the process of recovery.
- Remember, recovery is **two steps forward and one step back.** And the two-step forward period will get longer and longer, while the one-step back gets less and less frequent.
- Postscript: Mood changes can occur over days, as described above, but they can also occur over minutes or hours. One minute you may feel calm, the next enraged, the next sad, and so on.

The Raw Emotional Aftereffects: Extreme Anxiety

- We all live with a general, ongoing anxiousness about our everyday problems, but post-trauma anxiety is entirely something else. It is way off the charts. Panic is the most severe version of this.
- Some of this anxiety is a result of the states of hyper-arousal talked about earlier.
- However, extreme anxiety is more often connected with the sensation that you are in danger. You feel that a crisis is imminent—that at any moment danger could befall you.
- A pre-trauma world that seemed safe no longer exists. It will take some time for you to once again trust that the world is usually a safe place. When this occurs, the anxiety will lessen.

TWO RESPONSES TO THE RAW EMOTIONS

CONSTRICTION

- **Constriction** and **numbing** are two other common emotional reactions to trauma. They are both attempts to control the raw emotions.
- **Constriction** can affect action, emotion, thought, and perception. For example:
    - You were mugged in a grocery store so you don't go to them now.
    - You attempt to stop your tears when you recall the trauma.
    - You refuse to think about the event when it pushes into your mind, so you change subjects or do a chore.
- Constriction can narrow your world dramatically. This leads to not being able to lead your life in the way you did previously. Constriction has a way of feeding on itself. For instance, you stop going to grocery stores, but then you realize it could also happen in other kinds of stores, so you stop going to clothing stores and book stores and auto parts stores, and finally you just stay home.
- So, even though constriction may make you feel safe in the beginning, in the long run it can be debilitating. It is usually better to find other ways to manage and face your terror.

Jim, who had the bicycle accident, and Judie, who had the car accident, and Shawnee, who was carnapped, were all terrified to return to the places where their traumas occurred. Jim was fearful of riding again, Judie was terrified of driving, and Shawnee was terrified of the city and of the gas station where she was almost abducted. Each of them said that, by far, the hardest thing to do was to go back to those places, to get on that bike, to drive on that freeway, to go to that gas station. But they did it. Rather than constrict their lives by avoiding those scary places, they eventually faced their terror. Shawnee did it with help from a professional, who accompanied her to the actual scene of the crime. Judie did it with her "self-talk" method. And Jim did it carefully and cautiously. They all have their lives back as close as possible to what they were before the trauma because they were able to take those steps.[4]

NUMBING

- **Numbing** is mostly an attempt to deaden the feelings.
- Numbing can be dangerous because, often when you have been traumatized, you try to numb yourself with alcohol, drugs, excess activity, vegging out by watching TV, or playing computer games.
- These types of numbing are only as good as the minutes they last. As long as you keep drinking or using drugs or racing through your life, you will be successful in not feeling the feelings.
- But as soon as the alcohol or drugs wear off, or as soon as you slow down (or are forced to slow down through exhaustion or failing health), all those lousy feelings will still be there.
- It is best to try to avoid numbing yourself in these ways.
- The sooner you allow yourself to feel the effects of the trauma, the sooner you can resolve it.

Depression

   🍃 Depression is very common in the aftermath of trauma.

   🍃 It usually isn't experienced until some time has passed. Immediately after the trauma there is often a lot to do, and this can camouflage depression. But when activity subsides, you begin to feel depressed.

   🍃 Feelings of depression often are the result of the losses that accompany the trauma. Many of these losses have already been mentioned. For instance:

       • There is the loss of control accompanied by feeling small.

       • There is the loss of belief in the world as predictable and reliable.

       • There is the loss of mobility owing to physical injury.

       • There may be the loss of home and family and job.

   🍃 You are experiencing symptoms of depression if you notice you feel sad, lethargic, uninterested in life (especially in anything pleasurable), powerless, helpless, weighted down, unable to mobilize yourself, fatigued, diminished self-regard, or suicidal.

   🍃 You have reason to be depressed. Losing control of your life is depressing, and there are no two ways about it. Sometimes, however, it is also because a trauma can trigger unfinished business from the past.

❧ If you have never experienced these feelings, you may feel alarmed and wonder what is happening to you. Or if you have been depressed in the past, have overcome it, and now are experiencing it again, you may worry that your old depression is reemerging. Take heart! More often than not, depression caused by trauma is temporary.

- Depression is often alleviated when:
  - Mourning is completed.
  - Your usual way of living has been restored.
  - You have completed the other steps to resolution talked about later.

❧ Depression that persists should be treated through counseling and/or medication.

> *Actress Kelly McGillis said she had many years of depression and feelings of wanting to give up. Now, more than a decade after she was assaulted and raped, she says, "Be patient . . . you're not going to die. In moments of despair we look at everything as being so final. Assure people they won't die from it."[5]*

CHAPTER EIGHT

Everything Is Questioned

She's actually quite robust, and yet there is a childlike quality about Shawnee. She has an enthusiasm for life, for people, for love. Even after her experience.

Culver City, California, the home of MGM and other movie well-knowns, is not what one would think of as a high-crime area. So Shawnee, sitting in her Toyota truck in a gas station, waiting for her turn at the pump in this west-side suburb of Los Angeles at 2:30 in the afternoon, had no reason to be wary, nor to be conscious of what was going on around her.

And Shawnee, because she was friendly and trusting and had a spirit of goodwill, responded naturally when the man walked up to her open driver's side window and said hello. He asked her if she needed directions. His conversation stopped her from noticing another man at the passenger door. She had the windows down in her non-air-conditioned truck on this first day of September.

It wasn't until the gun was pressing into her side that she realized there was someone to her right. She turned to the friendly man with whom she had been speaking, thinking he would be an ally, and said, "That guy's got a gun." The friendly man told her, "Yeah, he's got a gun. Just do what he says." She froze—"Like a statue.

Nothing would come out of my mouth, nothing would come out."

The man on her right opened the passenger door, pushed his way in, and turned off the ignition, while the man on her left grabbed the steering wheel and began pushing the truck away from the pump area, where she had been waiting her turn. They commandeered her truck with her in it. The two men spoke loudly to each other, acting as if she needed help with her truck and making it seem as if they were coming to her aid so that others in the gas station would not be alerted.

What occurred next must have given her abductors their moment of panic. The man who had turned the ignition off had turned it one click too far. The steering wheel was locked, making the car unsteerable and unstoppable. It was rolling down an incline. The whole event had now taken on a life of its own, apart from the three of them, dragging them along until the truck slammed into the side of a parked car. The three of them again went into action. The gunman fled. The other man reached in and grabbed Shawnee's purse. She was moving that day and had just come from the bank, withdrawing cash for the movers. She did not want this man to take her purse. She wrestled him for it. She gave him a pretty good fight, but she lost. He left with her purse. She became hysterical.

Through her hysteria, Shawnee heard a woman screaming at her. It was the woman whose car the truck had run into. She was ranting and screaming accusations that Shawnee was part of an insurance scam, and Shawnee, through her hysterical terror, was trying to explain to her that the man had a gun and that she thought she was going to be killed. The car owner finally realized Shawnee's terror as authentic and backed off.

Two witnesses helped move her truck away from the car to pacify the owner. The police arrived and told Shawnee she should have her truck towed as soon as possible because the perpetrators had taken her keys and might return. Upon arriving home, she was faced with the details of insuring her safety, including reporting her stolen credit cards and having the locks changed on her doors. She realized she was too upset to work, so she canceled her appointments and called friends to let them know what had happened.

The first night brought the realization that sleeplessness and terror were going to be her bedfellows. She struggled for several days with the fear of falling asleep. When sleep did come, it brought nightmares and violent dreams in which she was chased by "black guys with guns." She also developed a skittishness and a nervousness, and a shrinking of her body when she walked down the street and saw black faces. And Shawnee, a child of the light, with a heart of goodwill, started having racist thoughts and became dismayed at discovering this about herself. The dreams didn't stop, the skittishness didn't stop, and the racist thoughts didn't stop. Her insurance company encouraged her to seek help. At first, she hadn't thought that she needed it, but she finally figured she may as well take advantage of the therapy for which the insurance company was going to pay. She went for a few sessions and then, thinking she was totally over it, stopped.

Two months later, it was Halloween. She answered the knock at her door. Before her were two black men in their thirties, costumed in shower caps, housecoats, and slippers, trick-or-treating. "I totally flipped out. Slammed the door. I called a friend, telling her about them. I was sure they were going to attack me. I was sure they had guns."

Shawnee paused, looked at me, and tongue-in-cheek said that when that happened she realized that she wasn't quite over it. She went back to the psychiatrist. The psychiatrist referred her to a psychologist who dealt in post-traumatic stress syndrome. The psychologist wanted her to go back to the gas station where it happened. Shawnee wasn't in any rush to go along with that suggestion, but finally agreed and the time was arranged for her and the psychologist to go together. The experience was terrifying for her because she was convinced that the men who had accosted her would come back to the station the very moment she was there. She kept telling the therapist she really wasn't comfortable doing this, but she persevered. Shawnee is grateful to the psychologist and herself, because it was one of the most helpful steps in her recovery.

Another helpful step was that she took a self-defense class. She discovered that her involuntary response to threat was to freeze. The instructor put her into situation after situation that replicated the sudden shock of being attacked, until she was able to respond differently.

Shawnee, this child of light who has a picture of Gandhi in her house, took a gun class. It convinced her not to buy a gun, but it also helped remove the mystique of guns. She's not afraid of guns now. It helped her understand how they work.

> *Shawnee feels recovered. And she feels changed. Permanently. The world is different. She used to believe her good-heartedness protected her and surrounded her with a protective "white light." She doesn't believe that anymore. She knows that anyone can be overtaken and killed. She describes herself as having lost her innocence and illusions, and that she has become cynical. The saddest part for her has to do with that cynicism because Shawnee believes that if you close yourself down to anyone then you close yourself down to everyone. She doesn't like to live that way, she didn't plan to live that way, but now, in order to feel safe, it is the only way for her to live.[1]*

☙ Because the thinking and perceiving aspects of your mind have been disrupted, **three areas come into question** during the period of disarray.

- Views of **yourself** come into question.
- Views of the **world** come into question.
- The **meaning of the trauma** as it relates to you and the world come into question.

☙ You question everything.

You Question Yourself: The Upside of Self-blame

- **Self-blame** is one way you question yourself. There is an upside and a downside to self-blame.
- The **upside** of self-blame is as follows:
  - It can be disconcerting to believe you were blameless in the trauma, because it means facing a chaotic and random world where anything can happen.
  - It can be more comforting to believe you are wrong than that the world is wrong.
  - In so doing, you achieve the illusion of control.
  - If you believe it was your behavior that caused the trauma, then you can believe you can change your behavior and thereby avoid trauma.
  - This can be comforting, but it's more than that. It also gives you a chance to assess whether you can do something now to protect yourself in the future.
  - Through self-blame, sometimes you can take precautions that will minimize the chance of harm in the future.
  - For instance, if you were in an earthquake and hadn't earthquake-proofed your home, you could do it now. Self-blame of this sort can lead to responsible action.

You Question Yourself: The Downside of Self-blame

❧ The **downside** of self-blame is as follows:

- If you perceived yourself as the cause of your trauma, you may not recognize the real danger. This could leave you in constant jeopardy.
- When you are harmed by another person, self-blame may not allow you to feel angry toward that person. Anger can help you feel in charge, and feeling in charge can be healing. When self-blame interferes with this, it is to your disadvantage.
- Others may find it difficult to offer help when you blame yourself. This can be a tremendous blow to your recovery because you need the help and attention of others.
- You may find it difficult to seek help, thinking you don't deserve it.
- Survivor guilt is another form of self-blame. This is when you feel others have suffered more than you, and you feel responsible for the inequity. This is an unnecessary burden.

Kelly McGillis blamed herself for years: "What did I do to cause this? I hated myself. I did bad things to myself. I just felt so shitty for so long about myself . . . it affected everything. [But] at some point I got to 'I didn't do it,' and realized we teach our children as little girls that anything sexual that happens to them, they're in control. But that's not true in rape, [where] it's random and violent ."[2]

You Question the World

- If you are not to blame, then you are left **questioning the world.**

- A professor of psychology, Ronnie Janoff-Bulman, has studied how our basic assumptions about the world are thrown into question following a traumatic event.[3]

- As she points out, most of us are unprepared for a traumatic event. We haven't thought of our world as a place where bad things can happen.

- So when they do happen, we just don't know what to think.

- Somehow, we have to figure out how this event can fit into the way we think about the world.

- Part of the task of feeling whole again is to fit a new puzzle piece into our pre-trauma puzzle. That means an old puzzle piece has to be put aside, left out, to make room for the new piece.

- Usually, this new piece has to do with accepting, in some way, that bad things can happen and do happen.

- Accepting that means you are permanently changed. It also means you are on your way to resolving the trauma.

You Question the Meaning of the Event

- We all attempt to explain the events that occur in our lives.
- Making sense of these events is something we need to do to believe our world has meaning.
- Although it may be difficult to figure out the meaning of the trauma in your life, it is generally . . .
  - Something that occurs almost without your trying. That is, you'll notice yourself spontaneously thinking about the reasons for the event.
  - Something that is necessary for a feeling of resolution about the trauma.
- Generally, thinking about the meaning of the event begins at the beginning of the healing process and ends at the end of it.
- Therefore, you may think of the meaning of the event in one way soon after and in other ways farther down the road.
- The way an event is interpreted is highly individual—there is no right or wrong way to assign meaning to the trauma.

CHAPTER NINE

The Reactions of Others

The hurricane struck South Florida on August 23, 1992. It was named Andrew. We all know about it, but probably not the way Tom knows about it. First, he knows about it because he was in it. Second, he knows about it from the point of view of a caregiver. Third, he knows about it as a member of a spiritual community, a community that stayed together during the hurricane and has remained together since.

Tom is a veterinarian. Prior to the big wind, many animals were brought to his clinic by frantic owners who were being evacuated from their homes and were not allowed to bring the animals to the shelters where they would be staying. Tom was hesitant to board them because he didn't know if the clinic was safe. As it turned out, he was still regretting that decision when I spoke with him a year later, because Tom's clinic was almost totally destroyed and many animals died in the hurricane. There was no way he could have known, but that doesn't seem to console him very much.

He was consoled, however, by the opportunity to provide emergency health care in shelters that were established just for the animals injured in the hurricane. This helped the animals and it helped Tom. It helped assuage the guilt he felt for his decision to accept the animals into his clinic before the storm. It also gave him the experience of working with some exceptional people. "It was the best experience. It was incredible to see. We've seen the worst that people can be and the best that people can be. It was just thrilling to see the best. It reminded me of M*A*S*H episodes. It was wonderful."

This was one of the two experiences that Tom had as a result of Hurricane Andrew that has to do with the all-important reactions of others. It was healing for Tom for them all to work together. It helped him work off the guilt he was feeling from the loss of the animals, but it seemed to be even more than that. It seemed to have to do with the strength that came from joining together, from being a unit. They could do something together that they could not do alone. It gave them a way to correct and reconstruct that which had gone wrong and had been destroyed. No one person could have accomplished even a small amount of what they did together. They were strong in number.

The other way was through what he experienced by being part of a spiritual community. Half of this community spent the hurricane night together after taking hours to move valuable equipment to safe places. Just being together helped. It was in the hours and days and weeks and months that followed, however, when he really experienced the way in which it helped to be part of this community. He first noticed the change when he went to his apartment and found every material possession gone. He felt like a load had been lifted from him as he recognized the meaninglessness of those possessions. He was without anything, even food and water for a while. And yet Tom felt an abun-

> *dance because he had what was important,*
> *which was his life and his friends and mutual*
> *support. He said it was a period of enlighten-*
> *ment that he has been able to maintain. He feels*
> *recovered and feels he doesn't have any baggage.*
> *He said it's because of the support he had. Even*
> *today, if he finds himself feeling upset, he has a*
> *community of people to whom he can turn. He*
> *is grateful.*[1]

- The reactions of others can mean the difference between healing or not!
- This may seem like a strong statement, and you may wonder if it is really so, but it is.
- People are dependent on other people for many things. However, during the post-trauma period, you may be extremely dependent.
- Recall that during this period you may feel small.
- For children, the opinions and attitudes of others mean everything in terms of how they feel about themselves.
- You are just as vulnerable as a child. The trauma has made you so.
- In the next few pages, I talk about what doesn't help and what does help in terms of the reactions of others.
- What follows really applies at any point during the post-trauma period, so it may be something to refer to more than once and at different times along the post-trauma road.

What Does Not Help

❧ A very frequent response that does not help is **blaming you.** This occurs for various reasons and has various effects.

❧ The reasons are:

- Blaming can make others feel nothing will happen to them. They can conclude you were traumatized because of your poor judgment or irresponsible behavior, rather than because the world is an unpredictable place where random events occur.
- It is better to believe you could have done something to prevent the trauma. This makes people feel safer and helps them control their own fears and feelings of helplessness about frightening events.

❧ The effects are:

- Blaming you isolates you by creating guilt. This leaves you feeling bad, confused, and ashamed. All of this leads to retreat.
- Blaming also disguises reality. The reality is that traumas do happen. The further reality is the majority of traumas are unavoidable because of how suddenly they occur. Only in the case of some types of natural disasters is there time to prepare.

❧ If those close to you are blaming you, you may want to . . .

- Find other people to support you who do not blame you.
- Educate those close to you about the negative effect of blaming you by having them read the section of this book written for them.

æ **It also does not help . . .**

- To have people try to talk you out of your feelings—for example, "Oh, you shouldn't feel that way."
- If someone will not listen to you. You need others to listen because you may need to go over the event repeatedly—it is one way to try to make the event be a part of your life, to fit that new puzzle piece into the big picture.

> *A woman woke up to find a burglar in her room. She had a delayed recovery that she attributed to a lack of trusting support. "I still have nightmares about intruders. I didn't have anybody to talk to about it at the time, so I wasn't able to get it out of my system. I really didn't have people whom I trusted enough to tell about my feelings then. I couldn't tell my family, so it was sort of bottled up. And I'm still carrying it around with me."[2]*

- To have people tell you to forgive whoever (or whatever) harmed you.
- For people to act as if nothing happened. This is known as the If-We-Don't-Talk-About-This-It-Will-Go-Away Syndrome. It's an illusion.
- To be told to put it in the past.
  - You know you would if you could, but trauma has a life of its own and usually insists on being remembered until it can be resolved.
  - Only when it is resolved can you put it in the past. Even then it is never erased—that is impossible. It happened and it will always exist.

- To have people minimize your experience. A trauma is a big deal.
- To be overprotected.
  - Protection is nice, but to be overprotected is to be made to feel like a baby.
  - You need to feel your wishes will be respected.
  - You cannot let someone run your life. You must be able to feel you are in control, that you are running the show called your life. This will help you feel your strengths and empower you, leading to recovery.

Lynn Manning did not want help. That was the hardest thing for other people to get through their heads. There is a word in the profession of psychology that fits Lynn's experience of how his family was treating him. They were infantilizing him—that is, they were treating him like an infant.

Granted, he needed some help for a while, but not anywhere near the help they all insisted upon. So eight months after his trauma, Lynn Manning moved into his own apartment, by himself, heaving a sigh of relief that he was no longer being hovered over. Before he moved, he took living skills classes. He learned about cooking and other basic skills. He also took a judo class.

In 1992, two weeks after the Olympics, Lynn Manning went to Barcelona, Spain, and participated in the Paralympics. The Paralympics are for the disabled. Lynn won the Silver Medal in judo. He is 100 percent blind.

Lynn looks like someone who could, hands down, win the Silver Medal in judo. He is 6'2" or slightly more. But it isn't his height that makes you know he's a winner. It's his stature. He is a presence, moving with a quiet, measured elegance befitting someone who must know his body from the inside out. He has built a strikingly well-balanced physique, a martial arts body with a hint of the weight lifter.

While it is Lynn's body that impresses first, it is his mind, his manner of expression, and his resplendent smile that impresses longest. These qualities have led to his other accomplishments. He does judo, yes, but in between writing poetry, writing plays, and more recently, acting.

Lynn did not do judo or write poetry or plays or act before the trauma that led to his blindness. He did other things, but not these things.

Lynn was blinded at twenty-three. He was shot through the left eye. The bullet went through his optic nerve and lodged in his skull on the right side. Even before being told by the doctors, he knew the bullet had blinded him. He wasn't surprised because he had been preparing for being blind since adolescence.

Lynn grew up in South-Central Los Angeles. Lynn saw grown-ups and children end up hurt and dead in South-Central L.A. Because of what Lynn saw and because he had become used to losing things that were important to him, he knew his chances were as good as anyone's for being a target.

Lynn began thinking about the worst that could happen to him. He was a talented painter. He realized the worst that could happen to him was to lose his eyesight. He had asked himself if he thought he could handle becoming blind. That was when he started to practice. He called it emergency training. He began dialing phones in the dark, tying his laces without looking, lighting cigarettes with his eyes closed, and not using lights in his home. During this time, he painted one of the two paintings I saw when I interviewed him: an eye that filled almost the entire canvas. In the circumference of the eye were eerie representations of birth and Father Time, which were painted as outgrowths of a graveyard. And from some outer area in space was a white sphere heading toward the eye, soon to penetrate it. It was a painting of what was to come.

He practiced being blind for many years before the Saturday night he went to a familiar Hollywood bar. The evening was unremarkable until a deranged patron began harassing Lynn. Finally, out of exasperation, Lynn threw the man out of the bar. Lynn went back into the bar and enjoyed another thirty minutes of socializing, but then the man returned with a gun.

Lynn's practicing and readiness were part of why he needed little help in those eight months before he went on his own. He was as ready as anyone could be. But his readiness had to do with something more. Lynn had a childhood in which any wish to depend on others had to be put aside. His biological father had left, followed by a string of surrogate fathers and foster homes, each ending abruptly. As Lynn said, he got used to losing what was important. These repetitive abandonments thwarted any chance for Lynn to depend on anyone, forcing him to become self-

reliant early in life. Lynn's frustrated wish for dependency is depicted in the second painting I saw before I left his apartment on the day we spoke. This painting is of a small boy sitting on the floor, with his arms wrapped around the leg of a man who is walking away. Undoubtedly, repeatedly being left would force one to become independent and to want to be the one who could walk away rather than be the one who was left behind.[3]

What Does Help

- You're probably wondering by now, **what does help?** In many ways, what does help is the opposite of what doesn't help.
- What helps the most is people who care and are able to address your needs.

Every day between July 14 and July 18, the McAlexanders had sixty to one hundred people helping them. Their house, located on four acres in the old section of Nebraska City, Nebraska, had been flooded by the overflow from the Missouri River. Everything had to be removed from the house, and by the end of the fifth day the house was clean enough (until they were flooded again four days later) to eat off the floor. Caring people provided hot food for two weeks, free goods to replace what was lost, hours of labor sorting through mud in the hope of finding precious collectibles, and the trailers, Dumpsters, and buckets to haul away what couldn't be saved. When I asked the beleaguered father of this household what advice he had for people who are traumatized, he advised, "Ask for help and take the free help that is given. I allowed people to come and help, and I was back in my house within days." And when I asked him what helped the most in their recovery, he instantly responded, "People helping was the best."[4]

  Caring people are people who . . .
- Can help provide a sense of safety.
- Can take over those things that you temporarily cannot do.
- Will spend the night with you if you need them.
- Will call the insurance company and the repair man and whomever else needs to be contacted as a result of the trauma.
- **Will listen to you.** This cannot be emphasized enough. It can be, by far, the most helpful thing someone can do for you.
- Will listen to you without judgment and without trying to change how you feel, and will respect what you say you need.
- Will ride the fluctuating wave of post-trauma feelings. "Go with the flow" might be a good motto for helpers.

  If you are fortunate enough to have caring people supporting you, remember to say thanks. Support your supporters with appreciation—it will help them be able to continue helping you.

"There's only one person who knows about it [the emotional effects of the accident] . . . a woman whose husband was injured on the job. Sometimes I just call her and dump . . . sometimes I cry. She understands and doesn't feel she has to do anything about it except listen. She's the only one I talk to about it." Cynthia and her handsome husband were in an auto accident. He was injured seriously and will never be able to fully walk again. Because of that their lives have changed dramatically.[5]

❧ **Information** provided by others is also very important.
- Information such as found in this book can help put your mind at ease.
- Information helps you to know that what you are experiencing is expected and that it will pass.
- More information is available through, for example, . . .
  - The Red Cross.
  - Additional reading.
  - Support groups.
  - Organizations.
  - Computer networks.
  - Government agencies.
- See Appendices A through E.

OTHER THINGS THAT CAN HELP

❧ Here's a **reminder** of some things previously mentioned that can help.
- Rest.
- Routine.
- A good diet.
- Exercise.
- Post-trauma counseling.
  - It may be necessary if . . .
    - You do not have a helpful group of supportive family and friends.
    - Your reactions persist even with support from family and friends.

❧ If you are concerned about the time and money for post-trauma counseling, it is usually short term and therefore should not be a great expense. There may even be free counseling available.

~ **Finally,** in this sometimes long middle phase, remember to:
- Stay away from people who can't help or don't help.
- Help educate people who are trying to help (give them this book).
- Keep in mind that you will go through changes and conflicting moods.
  - Some days you will want company, some days not.
  - Some days you will want to talk, others days you will not.
  - Some days you are going to be angry and sad, others just fine.
  - Be patient with these changes. They are part of putting the puzzle back together.

PART FOUR

Putting It into Place via Resolution

Resolve and thou art free.[1]

CHAPTER TEN

The Steps to Reorganization

❧ There are **four** things to keep in mind as you move into and through the resolution phase:

1. Even though it may not seem so, you will reach resolution. It is in the nature of people to move toward equilibrium, to a place of renewed balance. It is also in the nature of people to be resilient. In almost all cases, people bounce back.

2. Resolution may take longer than you think. Sometimes it may seem like you will never recover.
   • Keep in mind that there is, in general, a tendency for us to think we should be able to do things faster than we can, an impatience about being in a weakened condition, and a wish we could make things go faster than they can.
   • Healing has a mind of its own. There are actions you can take to aid in your recovery, but it will take as long as it takes.

3. Resolution is not removal.
   • The trauma happened. It will never go away.
   • Resolution is integration, which means making the trauma puzzle piece fit into a place that is a part of you.

4. Sometimes resolution is prolonged by external circumstances.
    - Victims of hurricanes, earthquakes, floods, or tornadoes often have to wait for resolution until rebuilding is completed. In some communities, that can take years.
    - People who have suffered physical injury sometimes go through recoveries that take months or years. This prolongs the journey of resolution.
    - If you were criminally victimized, you may be involved in legal proceedings that can also prolong recovery.

Kelly McGillis commented about her road to resolution that followed being raped: "It takes time to control yourself again, and that's the hardest time we as human beings have. We don't have patience. It takes time to deal with those feelings, to assimilate those emotions, and to overcome the pain and turn it into something positive as opposed to negative." [1]

The Goal of Resolution Is Reorganization

- All of the puzzle pieces have been thrown into disarray by the trauma.
- The puzzle pieces have to be put back into place for reorganization to occur.
- But they do not go back into place the way they were.
- Some new pieces have been added to this puzzle.
- The new pieces were created by the trauma.
- These are what has to be put into place in order for integration of the trauma to occur.
- To make room for the new pieces, some of the old ones must be left out of the puzzle.
- As it happens, those old ones wouldn't even fit anymore, even if you tried to fit them in because:
  - You have changed.
  - Your beliefs have changed.
  - Your experiences are different.
  - Maybe even your physical self has changed.
- So, the goal is to fit the new pieces in while giving up the old. How does this occur?
- There are several ways of arriving at the goal of reorganization. They are through:
  - Mourning.
  - Making words.
  - Acceptance.
  - Self-care and taking action.

THE IMPORTANCE OF MOURNING

- Mourning is one step toward putting the pieces of the puzzle into place.
  - Mourning means acknowledging and experiencing what you have lost.
  - Experiencing mourning means grieving.
  - Grieving means feeling deep pain about what you have lost.
  - What you have lost varies:
    - It can be the loss of another.
    - It can be the loss of physical capability.

Mike said after his permanently disabling auto accident: "I can't do most of what I could do before. I was very active, on my job, at home, with the kids. Sometimes I still try. It's eight months and I still have a hard time facing that I can't do what I used to."[2]

  - It can be the loss of property and valued possessions.
  - It can be the loss of financial stability.
  - It often is the loss of certain beliefs about the world.
  - It often is the loss of a sense of safety in the world.

- Mourning is the most difficult part of resolution.
- But mourning is necessary in order to go on.
- Mourning is necessary because . . .
    - It helps you let go of the old pieces.
    - If you try to hold on to the old pieces, you will find they don't fit.
    - If you can't make the pieces fit, you can't be whole again.
    - Fitting in the new pieces allows you to be whole again, to have all of the pieces of you in place.
- It is not unusual to fight mourning.
- No one wants to mourn because . . .
    - It is painful.
    - It can be momentarily debilitating.
    - It can bring up overwhelming and intense anger at having to face your losses and give up illusions. Having to face these painful realities is difficult enough. Having to feel the rage on top of it can feel like more than is manageable.
    - It temporarily makes you feel helpless again.
- Unfortunately, you have to mourn to move on, so it is better not to avoid it.
- Mourning won't last forever.

MAKING WORDS

❧ **Making words** is the second way of moving to resolution and putting that puzzle piece into place. Making words means being able to find words to describe the experience of the trauma.

- Trauma is an emotional and physical experience.
- The expression "blows your mind" is apt in describing trauma's effects because it is not a thinking experience.
- When trauma occurs, it is, instead, an experience of fragmented images and emotions.
- Finding the words to describe those images and emotions helps you capture the experience, helps you exercise control over it.
- Words help you to order and structure the chaos of trauma.
- Some people talk repeatedly about the trauma. In part, it is their effort to master the trauma through the use of words.
- Words are also the avenues to expressing the meaning of the trauma, which is an essential part of resolution.
- Finally, and most important, making words to describe the trauma *puts you in charge* of it.
- Being and feeling in charge of the trauma is one of the steps in the journey to resolution.

ACCEPTANCE

🍂 **Acceptance** is the next way you have of resolving the trauma and putting it into place. What exactly does acceptance mean, and how can it help with resolution?

- Acceptance is an aspect of mourning because it means accepting the losses.
- But acceptance is even more specific.
- It has to do with reality.
- The reality of traumas is that they happen to just about everyone.
- But that reality may be hard to accept.
  - Thoughts like "It's not fair" and "The world shouldn't be this way" crop up.
- It is true. It isn't fair, and ideally the world shouldn't be this way. But it is.
- Accepting this more realistic view can actually give you strength, as in the expression, "sadder, but wiser."
- But it isn't just sadder. Acceptance can also bring:
  - Calm.
  - More savvy.
  - More caution and prevention.
  - Confidence.

SELF-CARE AND TAKING ACTION

- ❧ These steps toward resolution come in many forms.
  - Some forms of self-care have already been mentioned, including meeting your physical needs, receiving support from others, and finding information.
  - The self-care discussed here has to do with something more. It has to do with taking stock.
  - It means looking at the trauma through a particular lens, the lens of responsibility.
  - Making a *realistic* assessment of your responsibility in the trauma will enable you to:
    - Take precautions in the future (if there are precautions to take).
    - Feel like you are in charge of your life in a way you were not before.
    - Feel some empowerment. That is, you can *do* something about averting or minimizing future trauma.
  - It is essential that you *realistically* assess what you may have been able to do differently, keeping in mind throughout that most trauma is:
    - Unpredictable.
    - Sudden.
    - Not something for which you can completely prepare.
- ❧ You are now ready to rethink what occurred.
- ❧ Go through the steps you can take to prevent or reduce the effects of trauma in the future:
  - Can you maximize the safety of your property?
  - Do you have first aid available in your home and car?
  - Have you contacted your local Red Cross and your Community Services officer for suggestions for emergency planning?

*Gwenne and her family were in Hurricane An-
drew. Her husband helped himself deal with his
depression and helplessness after Andrew by
buying supplies. Lots of them. Like fifty rolls of
toilet paper.*[3]

*Shawnee took action by enrolling in a self-
defense class after her assault. She said this was,
by far, the most helpful action she took in her
recovery.*[4]

☙ The possibilities for taking action are endless.

*In Stockton, California, a man came to a school
yard and started shooting. He killed five,
wounded twenty-nine others, and then killed
himself. This was a multiethnic community, and
in some cultures traditional mental health ap-
proaches were foreign and inappropriate and,
actually, not useful. Other more creative and in-
ventive ideas had to be used to help the children
who witnessed this massacre. Here is one example of a highly unusual action that worked.*

*"One little boy . . . complained of seeing ghosts
on the playground of the school. Although this
might have been interpreted by psychotherapists
as a potentially dangerous hallucination, his parents and other members of his community knew
better. He did not need drugs or counseling. . . .
It was the playground that needed exorcising.
With permission from school officials, the Ven-
erable Dharmawara Mahathera, a 100-year-old
Buddhist monk, came to the Cleveland School*

> *several weeks after the shooting to chant scrip-*
> *ture and sprinkle holy water on the spots where*
> *the children were gunned down. The ghosts dis-*
> *appeared."*[5]

ᵛ• A last note about taking action. I have spoken with many
people dislocated from their homes by natural disasters
and fires. Everyone said that what helped them most was
routine, routine, routine. The sooner they could return to
a normal routine, the better.

> *Gwenne, from Hurricane Andrew, said that her*
> *husband didn't show signs of his old self until*
> *just before I spoke with her—it was three weeks*
> *after the one-year anniversary of Andrew and*
> *three weeks after they had finally returned to*
> *their home. His unhappy disposition changed*
> *immediately once they were home. She finally*
> *had her husband back.*

> *Everyone who had children stressed how their*
> *children's behavioral changes disappeared, some*
> *entirely, once routine was established and nor-*
> *mality was returned. Obviously, we need order*
> *to feel safe, so any action that can be taken to-*
> *ward the establishment of routine is enthusias-*
> *tically recommended.*[6]

A Final Note About Resolution

- The hardest thing about this phase is waiting for it to be completed.
- Resolution takes time and, more often than not, **a long time**—sometimes even years.
- It is natural to become impatient. No one wants to feel the effects of trauma any longer than necessary. But, unfortunately, the pace of resolution is determined by forces beyond what we would wish. Healing has its own time clock.
- As best you can, be patient toward yourself and with the process of healing. It will make it easier if you can do so.

CHAPTER ELEVEN

Outcomes

Earnest, refreshing, inspiring, focused, changed.

This is Dan at twenty-two. This is Dan after the bomb. Dan is one of thousands who were trapped in New York's World Trade Center when the terrorists' bomb went off. He was at a graduation luncheon at the Windows on the World restaurant, on the 107th floor.

The commencement speaker had just said the word "heaven" (referring to their location in the building) when the explosion occurred. They heard it, Dan said, more than felt it, and everyone startled in anxious laughter. The speaker, in some way that Dan couldn't exactly remember, tied the sound to his speechmaking and everyone laughed more.

They didn't laugh when they heard the second boom. They wondered, nervously yet quietly, murmuring among themselves. Before they smelled the smoke, an order to evacuate came from building security. Napkins wetted with water were handed out and people were directed to the stairwell. As they began their descent, they saw smoke curling up toward them. When Dan becomes nervous, he talks. And he jokes—black humor. He realized not everyone was finding his jokes funny, so he stopped. In the stairwell, the talk continued. They speculated. But then they became more quiet. The seriousness of their cir-

cumstances was reluctantly invading their consciousness. Some people began to panic. Some
began to cry. Some began to shout, "Move it,
move it!" Others called for calm.

Did you know that napkins, wetted, don't
work? They're not porous enough. But, Dan
said, with a seasoned tone, "Breathing through
ties is good. And pieces of shirt torn away,
they're good."

Breathing became the new focus. "In through
your nose, out through your mouth." The focus
was "on keeping a steady pace and remaining
calm, so as not to use up too much oxygen."

The pace was frighteningly slow. It took two
and a half hours to descend from that 107th
floor. Two and a half hours is 150 minutes,
9,000 seconds. There was a lot of time to think.
The quieter it became, the more thinking Dan
did. What was the smart thing to do? Was going
along with the crowd the right move? Once in
a while, someone would come into the stairwell from one of the floors and Dan would find
himself looking out onto the floor, wondering if it would be better to "pull out on one of
these floors and just hold out." But, he said,
people were saying, " 'No, no, everybody stick
together!' I guess it was kind of like group men-
tality, like what the group says is right and whatever you're thinking is wrong, so you know, you
stuck with it. It's strange. When you're in a situation you've never been in before and people
are acting like they're in control, like they know
what's going on, you stick with the group. I
guess you're afraid to go with what you think
might really be right. Now, I think it would have
been smarter to just stay there . . . but hindsight
is twenty-twenty."

The smoke was thickening. People were shedding briefcases, jackets, all extra weight. For older people, breathing became labored. Quiet prevailed. It was solemn in that stairwell. And, then, at the 50th floor, the lights went out. Quickly, a system developed. One hand stretched to the person in front, keeping feet steady so as not to falter, they were a blind chain, going who knew where. They traveled thirty-five floors like this, chaining together, breathing together, pacing together.

Relief. Finally. Thank god. Firefighters in the stairwell at the 15th floor. Police officers. One or the other on each new floor. Assuring them. Telling them what their desperateness longed to hear. Thank god, we're going to be okay!

Daylight. Hugging, Raising commotion. Now what? Talk. A lot. With each other.

Dan said the real reflection began the next day. That's when he realized he could have died. He started to feel more of the emotions. And a new line of thinking began. "I guess you could say it was like a mid-life crisis at twenty-two. It was like a revival kind of thing, like there's just so much I wanted to do. What if it had ended then? I'm not ready. It was like a learning experience. Don't miss out on life while you can. And what would people think about me if I were gone? Would they miss me, would they say he was a good guy or he was a jerk? Would they just not care? What was the purpose, did I do anything to change anything? I've heard success is helping to improve the quality of someone else's life during your lifetime. I thought about that. Had I done that? Also, it was selfish. I didn't want people to think, 'Dan died, good. He was a jerk. He got what he deserved.'

"*I don't think that's all of it, but you do want your life to mean something. You want to be missed. I mean, you do. I wouldn't want someone to ruin their life over my dying, but I'd want them to cry at my funeral, to cry a little bit, kind of feel bad and then move on.*

"*All kinds of questions I tried to figure out. It was kind of difficult. I started thinking what could I do to get the most out of life. If I died in a year or two years, what could I do to make the most out of it?*"

Dan went overboard. He tried to do everything. He made big plans. He was going to do everything he had always wanted to do and thought he should do. He could die and it could be soon and he knew it, at twenty-two. He put that weight set out in the backyard, ready to pump iron. He wanted to contribute to the Wildlife Way Station because he loved animals. He thought about wanting to be a success at work, but he also thought about wanting to live life to its fullest, to live it in a balanced way. He thought about his wish to be more involved in team sports. He thought about how he was used to spending his time and if it was productive. He thought about his couch-potato, pool-playing, getting-smashed habits and how those and work were all he did. He made big plans to turn it around, to be more disciplined in his off-time and less a workaholic in his on-time.

He failed. He failed his own expectations. So he had to think some more. He had to come to terms with time. He felt he might not have enough time to do it all because now he knew he could die tomorrow. But he realized that everything takes time and there isn't time to do it all at once. He had to learn about letting go and *postponing and focusing and getting tired and planning, along with learning about living.*

He thought about it all. He made adjustments. He threw away the weight set (a relief, since he hated pumping iron). He became clever. He found one thing that would meet many needs: karate. It gave him the exercise he thought he should have, plus the focus and discipline he wanted for work and, finally, self-defense. The ability to defend himself had become important now that he had discovered vulnerability, knowing that anything can happen anytime. He also became the manager for his company's softball team. He let the Wildlife Way Station go, for now. He contacted old friends, expanding his social circle outside of the pool room. He told people he loved them. He made plans with them. And he found his life's philosophy, at least for now. It is to live for today, enjoy today, but always keep your eye on the future. Wisdom at twenty-two.[1]

There are five outcomes as a result of resolution:

- I have lost, but I am.
- Reevaluation of value and goals.
- Compassion.
- Social action.
- Permanent change.

Outcome 1:
I Have Lost, But I Am

🙦 This outcome is very much a result of mourning.

🙦 You have discovered, through mourning, that you can let go of the pieces that don't fit **and still be you.**

🙦 This recognition that the trauma did not destroy you is . . .
  - One of the most strengthening outcomes.
  - One of the most meaningful outcomes.
  - One of the most celebrative outcomes. In it, you can feel triumphant. **You** have not been beaten.

🙦 In my years of work with traumatized people, this realization is always a shining moment.

🙦 This is especially important if you were hurt by another human being. It means that person did not defeat **you.** The person may have harmed you, maybe even have done some permanent damage, but **you** have won in the end.

🙦 **You** are to be congratulated for being more than the event.

Gwenne is upbeat. Even a hurricane didn't get her down too much. She and her family were out of their home for an entire year. They had just enough to get by, and they waited as the long process of rebuilding and repair took place. In spite of this, Gwenne seemed to have a perspective because she knew what was really important. Her husband was important and her children were important. And, as difficult and taxing as it was to not have her home, she knew she had herself. Because she had that all along and all along kept her perspective, she was also able to accept the benefits of the experience. She was able to let go of what she had lost, relish her survival, and welcome the new.[2]

Outcome 2:
Reevaluating Values and Goals

🐦 It is common knowledge that most people reevaluate their values and goals when they come face-to-face with possible death.

🐦 You may find yourself looking around and wondering why you thought such and such was so important.

🐦 Suddenly, other things become important. Often, it is family and friends.

> *Adrian and Dede lived on the earthquake epicenter in Northridge, California. Their townhouse had been filled with collections of antiques. The quake reduced them by half. They emphatically stated they have no plans to replace them, because all that matters to them now are the people in their lives, not their belongings.[3]*

🐦 Or, it may be following that dream that you never seemed to pursue.

> *Kelly McGillis said, "You have to go on, you have to grow. It makes you wiser in the long run; you can use it. I've been able to make my experience a positive in terms of my thinking and my viewing life and viewing how I raise my kids."[4]*

🐦 Whatever its focus or form, it points out that trauma will, at least, change your life and it is hoped, enrich your life.

Outcome 3:
Compassion

- More than likely you have been humbled by the trauma.
- It has made you aware of . . .
  - Your vulnerability.
  - Your mortality.
  - Your need for others.
- This often leads to a new sensitivity to others.
  - If you have always been that tough macho man, you may find yourself having softer feelings than before.
  - If you have had trouble allowing yourself to be close and expressive with those you care about, you may find it's a little easier and is something you desire.
  - If you were impatient with others during their difficult times, you may notice you have a newfound patience.
- Compassion is another outcome that is hard won, but can be life-altering and life-enhancing.

Outcome 4:
Social Action

- Many people experience more energy as a result of resolution.
- They often direct that energy toward prevention of future traumas like the one they experienced.
- One of the best-known examples is Candy Lightner, the mother who began MADD (Mothers Against Drunk Drivers) after losing a child in an accident caused by a drunk driver.
- Often, this kind of social action is a way to give meaning to the loss.
- It is also a way to develop purpose in one's life after another purpose has been ripped away.

> *A reporter talked about the parents of Rebecca Schaeffer. She was the young actress on* Sister Sam *who was fatally shot. "And in mourning their daughter's lost life, [her parents] have resumed theirs with a new sense of purpose. Once relatively apolitical, they have become leaders in Oregon's gun-control movement."*[5]

  Social action creates empowerment, focus, purpose, meaning, and repair—all of which lead to healing and recovery.

Outcome 5:
Permanent Change

  No matter what the trauma, it brings permanent change.

  This is an outcome that is inevitable.

  Unlike the other outcomes, this one is universal.

  For some, the change may be small. For others, it may permeate their lives.

> *Dorothy, who was in Hurricane Andrew, said, "We will never ever again be complacent to a hurricane season."*[6]
>
> *Kelly McGillis, who was raped in her apartment, said, "I don't think I've ever felt safe since, in a home or in a hotel. I never have taken safety for granted again. And, I'm much more cautious. You learn to protect yourself and take responsibility for protecting yourself."*[7]
>
> *Shawnee, the child of the light, doesn't trust the way she did. She is cautious and skeptical and questioning . . . her blinders are off.*[8]

  All of the people with whom I spoke told me the same thing: life is different now. It is the same for everyone—there is a permanent difference.

CHAPTER TWELVE

Professional Help

- ❧ How do you know if you need professional help to reach resolution?
- ❧ There are certain criteria that you can use to help you make this decision.
    - If you do not have a good and caring support system via family or friends, you may be more likely to need professional help. Most people cannot deal with trauma entirely on their own.
    - If you see your reactions to the trauma are persisting, seek professional help.
    - If you see there are certain things about you that have changed and have remained that way, seek help. For example, if you have improved in every way, but are constricted from going to the grocery store (because you were mugged in a grocery store), you probably need help.
    - Families are often deeply affected by a family member being traumatized. It affects everyone. If your family is not recovering, seek help for the family.
- ❧ Try not to postpone finding professional help. The longer you wait, the longer the reactions persist, the longer it will take you to recover.

Grief shared is grief diminished.[1]

Blocks to Seeking Professional Help

- Often, the social climate in which you live does not support seeking help because it is sometimes thought to be a sign of weakness, a sign of shame that you can't help yourself.
  - **However, it is not a sign of weakness to seek help. It is quite the opposite. It is a sign of taking charge of the trauma. It is no different from taking a broken leg to a medical doctor.**
- You may also feel that seeking help is a sign that you are still helpless, as you were during the trauma.
  - **However, it does not mean you are still helpless. In fact, you risk remaining helpless if you do nothing. Again, seeking help is taking charge.**

> *After being raped, Kelly McGillis postponed seeking help for a long time. "I just didn't sleep for two years. There was no way I would go to sleep at night, and finally I realized I'm going to kill myself from not sleeping so I better go see somebody." She did go and after a short time was able to sleep and discontinue therapy.*[2]

- You may believe that talking about it will make it worse, so you and those around you promote the "just forget about it" attitude.
  - **Talking about it and facing it will not make it worse. Instead, it will give you a chance to understand what it has meant to you and how it is affecting you so you can put it into perspective.**
- You may fear you just won't know how to talk about it or you won't be understood.
  - **A good post-trauma counselor will know how to help you talk if you are having trouble.**

◆ You may fear that having feelings about the trauma is "silly" or "stupid" or "abnormal," so you would find it embarrassing to have someone know you had such feelings.

  • It would be a surprise if you did not feel this way. Trauma is upsetting, that's just all there is to it. A trauma counselor should not be surprised or judgmental about your feelings.

The following is about a Midwest flood victim: "A burly blue-collar worker broke down at a Red Cross center, and his troubles cascaded out: He had lost his home and his job and was unable to tell his wife how bad things were because she had epilepsy and he feared she would not be able to bear it. The two of them were holed up in a motel room with their three young children, and he did not know how much more he could take. A social worker guided him to a back room to talk.

"His eyes were filled with tears by the time we sat down. I told him, just go ahead and cry, and he did. He just cried and cried and cried. He cried for about fifteen minutes. He kept saying, 'I don't even know who you are, and here I am crying like a baby.' And I kept saying, 'You are not the first.' "[3]

Forms of Professional Help

ɜ There are several types of professional help. These include:

- **Individual counseling:** It is preferable to find a
  counselor or therapist who has experience working with post-traumatic stress disorder (PTSD).
  This is because PTSD has certain symptoms that
  are treated in a certain way and it is important
  your counselor or therapist is able to recognize
  those symptoms and knows how to treat them.
  Usually, this type of treatment is short-term. It
  may become long-term if the trauma has led to
  the uncovering of earlier difficulties that were dor-
  mant until the trauma stirred them up. It's like the
  proverbial lid being blown off. If this occurs, you
  will then need long-term help. If you cannot find
  someone who is familiar with PTSD, suggest to
  your counselor that he or she familiarize themselves with PTSD by reading this book and the lit-
  erature on treatment.
- **Support groups:** There are often support groups
  available for specific types of trauma. For example,
  groups for women who have been raped, groups
  for victims of criminal assault, groups for disaster
  victims and so on. It is best if these are professionally run groups. More often than not these groups
  will be time-limited, that is for a specific number of
  weeks. Most people find it extremely helpful to talk
  with other people who have gone through what
  they have.
- **Medication consultation:** This should be sought if
  you are struggling with sleep-related problems,
  with overwhelming intrusions or emotional flood-
  ing, or with extreme anxiety and/or panic attacks.
  A medication consultation is best done with a psychiatrist rather than a general practitioner. This is

because psychiatrists specialize in knowing about these types of medication. It is even better if you can locate a psychiatrist who specializes in using medication to treat PTSD. You can begin your search for someone by contacting the American Psychiatric Association.

- **Self-help groups:** There may be self-help groups in your area. The advantage of these is that they are usually no cost. However, they are only recommended if you are doing pretty well and just need a place to meet others who have gone through the same experience. Keep in mind, if you are having a really tough time you probably need more than a self-help group. That is the time to turn to a professional.

- **Combination of group and individual therapy:** Group counseling can be very useful if you are seeing a therapist individually and want to also have the chance to speak with others who have gone through what you are going through. The combination of individual therapy with the support of a group (professionally led or self-help) can be very powerful. You can seek either a professionally run group or a self-help group to use in combination with your individual therapy. You may want to discuss this with your individual therapist to determine the best time to go into a group and to have your therapist recommend a group.

CHAPTER THIRTEEN

Some Take Longer

> It took Kelly McGillis years to recover: "I'm not
> innocent [now] in many ways. Some of it is [the
> rape]. I'm using the lessons from that, using them
> in a positive, constructive manner as opposed to
> a hateful, destructive manner. Your first re-
> sponse is the childish thing and then you move
> into the adolescent level of being angry and re-
> bellious about it and then the adult level of O.K.,
> it happened, it wasn't my fault, things happen to
> people, I'm going to carry on. Time . . . that's
> most healing, time. It took me years."[1]

- There are many reasons why some people take longer to
  recover than others.
- They include . . .
    - The degree of threat, intensity, and loss from the
      trauma.
    - Whether the trauma was caused by people or na-
      ture.
    - The extent of your support system and how impor-
      tant people in your life react to you after you have
      been traumatized.
    - Whether your physical abilities changed and your
      roles in life changed.
    - The kind of personality you had before the trauma.
    - How you were coping before the trauma.
    - Whether you had been previously traumatized.

- If you were traumatized as part of a group or you were alone.
- The way you reacted during the trauma.
- Secondary gains.

Threat, Intensity, and Loss

Not all traumas are alike in threat and intensity and loss. For instance,

- Traumas that last longer take longer to resolve.
- Traumas that have more threat of death take longer to resolve.
- Traumas that involve loss of irreplaceable property take longer to resolve.
- Traumas that involve the loss of loved ones take longer to resolve.
- Traumas that have persistent reminders take longer to resolve.

Earthquakes have this nasty quirk called aftershocks. You never know when the next one will be and you never know if it's of life-threatening proportions. Andrea was in her kitchen trying to clean up from the first shock. She heard the aftershock before she felt it. It was one of the biggest, and in that moment she wished she could will herself to die. She just didn't want to go through it again, especially not knowing when (or if) it was ever going to end.[2]

When a Person Causes the Trauma

&. Traumas that are inflicted by a person rather than an act of nature often are more difficult to resolve.

- For some, being traumatized by another person brings into question the existence of evil in the world. It is hard to come to terms with the existence of evil people.

- Being traumatized by another makes you wonder why *you* were chosen over someone else. It makes it feel more personal, that it had something to do with you, that it was your fault.

- Being traumatized by another carries a stigma with it. Somehow, you feel "marked," whereas others are not.

- There often is a severe breakdown in trust of others when you have been hurt by another person. This prolongs recovery.

- There is a tendency, when a person has caused the trauma, to begin to respond to all people who have the characteristics of the person who caused the trauma as if they, too, will traumatize you. Therefore, if you were assaulted by a tall, blond man with a beard who wore a red plaid flannel shirt and denim jeans you may find yourself reacting to all men with these characteristics. From this may grow a tendency to stereotype and you will find yourself thinking prejudicial thoughts about this type of person. This can be disturbing if you have not considered yourself to be a prejudiced person. All of this leads to it being more complicated to undo the effects of the trauma.

The Support-System Factor

ৡ If, following the trauma, you are unable to depend on others around you, the resolution may take longer.
  - If family and friends cannot support you, you may feel more isolated.
    - Isolation can lead to withdrawal.
    - Withdrawal can lead to loss of contact with others.
    - Contact with others is necessary as an outlet for expression as well as support.
  - Government agencies that are responsible for reimbursement so that people can rebuild can be inefficient. This leads to isolation, frustration, and disillusionment and can prolong recovery.
  - Those traumatized by natural disasters often feel deserted after receiving help from outside groups, such as the Red Cross. Such organizations are there in the beginning, but then they leave. The feelings from this felt sense of desertion are unresolved anger, futility, and isolation.

The Physical Change and/or Role Change Factor

ৡ If the trauma led to a change in your physical ability and/or your role at home and work, the trauma may take longer to resolve.
  - Temporary or permanent physical injury can affect aspects of your recovery. For example:
    - It affects mobility. Being mobile makes you feel less helpless.
    - Not feeling helpless enables you to overcome helplessness.

- It affects your self-esteem. If you feel crummy about yourself, it is difficult to overcome the effects of the trauma.
- The same is true if your role in your family or at work or at play has been affected.
  - If suddenly you can no longer do what you were used to doing, you may feel worthless.
  - If others have to take over what you used to do, you may feel displaced. Your life's purpose has been affected, leaving you floundering and confused.

Who You Were Before the Trauma

- Who you were before the trauma can make a difference in resolving the trauma.
- If your life was running smoothly and you felt pretty optimistic about yourself and the world, you are more likely to recover sooner. You'll most likely still be affected, but not for as long. But . . .
  - If you had life problems that were unresolved, a trauma will just add to the stress you were already under.
  - If the trauma was in addition to a history of childhood abuse and/or other difficult childhood experiences and these had not been resolved, your recovery will most likely be more difficult.
    - For some, the trauma may bring those childhood experiences back to the surface, so that you are left with double traumas to face.
  - If pre-trauma you were without support systems, you are more likely to have difficulty recovering.
    - It is *very* important, if you are isolated, to hook up with helping people. Doing this will aid tremendously in your recovery.
  - If, prior to the trauma, you were coping with other losses, your recovery may be longer.

The Prior-Trauma Factor

- ❧ Sometimes, prior traumatic experiences can make a difference.
- ❧ This can go in two directions.
- ❧ For some, a prior experience can make the next one more difficult.
  - You may not have fully recovered from the first trauma, so it is more akin to being knocked down again before ever really having a chance to get back on your feet.
- ❧ For others, a prior trauma can make the next one less difficult.
  - They may have been toughened up in certain ways as a result of the trauma.
  - Some people report that a prior trauma made them feel stronger after going through it.
  - Others say they learned to take preventive measures, thereby minimizing the effects of future traumas and feeling less guilt because of the caretaking they had done.
  - For others, it seems to be easier because they realized that sometimes bad things happen in the world. Therefore, they find themselves feeling more accepting of subsequent traumas because they fit their expectations.

Liz told me about her reaction to her daughter's trauma and how it differed from the reactions of her two other daughters. Liz said they weren't so sure everything was going to be okay, but she never had a doubt. Her daughters cried a lot, while she was stoic.

> *Then, as though she was having the realiza-*
> *tion at the moment she was speaking to me, she*
> *said, "Maybe I am stoic—maybe it's because I've*
> *gone through some horrific things myself. I think*
> *as you live your life you become an acceptor and*
> *a fighter.*
>
> *"I know how fragile I am and how fragile*
> *you are. We're all very fragile and we're all*
> *maybe that close to dying every time we take a*
> *step. And so you go around these things. There's*
> *strength in knowing you are fragile. And that*
> *your expectations are realistic."*[3]

The Group vs. Individual Factor

- If you were one among many who were traumatized, your recovery may be shorter than if you were the only one.
    - As part of a group, you are less likely to question whether it was your fault. Therefore, you don't have that added burden of conscience.
    - As part of a group, you have others with whom to share the experience. This can greatly reduce . . .
      • The chance of isolation.
      • The chance you won't receive support.
      • The chance of stigma.
    - As part of a group, you have a shared common goal that could take many forms, such as:
      • To fight back.
      • To rebuild.
      • To console.
      • To repair.
      • To prevent.

The Way You Reacted During the Trauma

- If, during the trauma, you behaved in such a way that later shocked you, it may take you longer to recover.
- There are situations when there may have been participation in victimizing others or when you didn't reach out with a helping hand. Such actions may overwhelm you following the trauma. You may wonder:
  - How could I have done such a thing?
  - What kind of a person am I?
  - Why didn't I behave more heroically, with more courage?
- **No one, absolutely no one,** can predict how he or she will behave in the fury of a traumatic situation. **You did what you did to survive.**
- If you have a prolonged struggle with the way you acted during the trauma, *get help*. There are ways to overcome this burden, both through processing the event and through action.

Secondary Gains

- Some people take longer to resolve their trauma because there may be benefits from not recovering. These benefits are called secondary gains. They may come from a variety of sources. For example:
  - There may be a lawsuit that has resulted from the trauma where it may seem more beneficial to remain symptomatic.
  - There may be insurance proceeds which end when recovery is completed.

- There may be a certain amount of attention you are receiving that is difficult to give up.
- There may be a job you dislike to which you would have to return once recovered.

  🍃 All these secondary gains may lead you to begin building an identity around being a victim. If this occurs, it then becomes difficult to imagine existing without your victim status. The benefits and the identity may be difficult to relinquish and therefore will prolong your recovery.

> *Actress Kelly McGillis talked about the secondary gains she found in herself. "It's very comforting to be a victim for the rest of your life. It's easy. It's a way to not live life; it's a way to not be engaged and live life. It's a way of hiding from life, and it took me a while to realize that. It's terrible, but it's comforting to be in pain. Happiness and joy, those are scary, new and freeing . . . it's scary."[4]*

A Few Last Words

  🍃 Overall, it is important to keep in mind that no two of you are alike.

- You come from different backgrounds.
- You have different personalities.
- You have different support systems.
- You suffered varying physical trauma.
- But, most important, your experience is yours alone, no matter how similar to others' the circumstances may be.

  🍃 **The key variables in your recovery are:**

- The type, intensity, and duration of the trauma.
- The type and amount of support from those around you.

PART FIVE

For Those Close to Someone Traumatized

All that will matter to you when you are old is how much you have loved.[1]

CHAPTER FOURTEEN

Your Reactions

Bud and Betty have been married since 1947. She had planned on being married a lot longer. But there was a stretch of time when it seemed it might not happen—about twenty-eight days, before they knew for sure he was going to survive the fall.

Bud and Betty's next-door neighbors had sandblasted their house. The sandblasters blew the residue into Bud and Betty's yard and driveway and onto their roof. Betty didn't think she would be able to stand all that sand coming into her house, so she asked Bud to clean it up. Bud had spent his career as a telephone repairman, so he was used to climbing and taking the necessary precautions to ensure his safety. He exercised those precautions this time as well, but he didn't realize that some of the sand he had cleaned off the roof had landed on the ladder. When he started his descent from the roof, his foot slipped and he fell flat on his back on the cement below. He thought he had broken both legs because he couldn't move. It turned out to be worse than that.

The hospital had difficulty making a correct diagnosis. During this time, Bud's condition worsened. He was in extreme pain. His screams could be heard throughout the ward and his bodily functions shut down. Betty feared the worst—she feared she was losing her husband. His condition worsened and her worry deepened, but finally, after almost a month, new and more definitive tests were ordered and it was realized that Bud's vertebra had shattered into his spinal cord. Now, not only did the screams make sense, but something could be done.

Bud was moved to another hospital where several surgeries were performed to remove the pieces of vertebra. After almost two months, Bud went home.

Betty's life had changed. Now she had a husband who was bedridden and needed extensive care. Before he left the hospital, Betty was taught how to move him and clean him and care for him. But she was not trained as a nurse. She had never done anything even remotely like this. She was scared. She was on her own. And she still had to go to work. Fortunately, a neighbor was able to check in on him during the day, but the majority of the care fell on Betty.

Betty often was up until two or three in the morning in order to accomplish everything that needed to be done. Taking care of Bud and her regular job absorbed her seconds, her minutes, her hours, her days. She had no time for any other activities or interests, including her participation in a singing group. Exhaustion characterized the thirteen months Bud was bedridden. In fact, even though it was years later, Betty sounded exhausted as she told me her story.

During this time, Bud was very demanding and would sometimes take her for granted. This was hard for her and she felt resentful and unappreciated. Usually when she reminded him he wasn't the only person in the house, it helped. He could see how stressed she was and would

*become appreciative again. Then it was better
for Betty. She would feel her resentment leave.
She said, though, that even during times of resentment, she forced herself to keep a smile. She
did that for him because if she was in a discour-
aged mood, he would detect it and become dis-
couraged himself.*

*Bud is out of that bed now. Not only is he
out, he is walking and doing and going. He isn't
100 percent yet, but that's okay with Betty. She's
grateful that she still has her husband. It would
have been lonely without him. There was no
question in Betty's mind about doing the caretaking. It comes with the package of loving
someone. Even though it may be exasperating,
exhausting, frustrating, and require setting aside
your own needs, you just do it.*[1]

You, Too, Are Affected

- If you are a relative, a friend, a spouse, a colleague or fellow worker, or in a role of authority to the person traumatized, you have been affected by the trauma.
- You will have your own reactions to and feelings about the trauma **and** to the one traumatized.
- And you will have a very important decision to make.
- That decision is whether you want to make yourself available to the person who was traumatized.
- This section is about your reactions, your feelings, and your decision to help or not help.
- It is also about what will and will not help *you*.
- Finally, it is about what will and will not help the one you are helping.

You, Too, Have Been Shocked

- It may be a surprise to you that **you are affected.**
- But if you stop to think about it, why wouldn't you be?
    - After all, you are an integral part of the person's life.
    - When someone who is close to you is affected, you are also.
- You are affected in ways similar to the person traumatized and in ways different from the one traumatized.
- **You, too, have been shocked by the trauma.**
- However, your shock is different because it doesn't include the physical part.
- You are not affected by hyperarousal, as is the person who was traumatized.
- Your shock is the kind that is experienced as, "I can't believe this happened to ———." Therefore, **disbelief** is your primary and initial reaction.
- You may find that at certain moments you can believe it and then you cannot.
- It is similar to the denial-intrusion cycle the traumatized person goes through, but the degree of intensity is less. It helps you experience the reality of the trauma in doses that you can manage.

YOUR ROUTINES HAVE BEEN CHANGED

- If the person traumatized sustained physical injury and is either hospitalized and/or going through rehabilitation, **your routines may be disrupted.**
  - You may be worried about the one you care for and this could affect your . . .
    - Sleeping.
    - Eating.
    - Exercising.
    - Working.
  - You may be making trips back and forth to the hospital and/or doctor or physical therapist or chiropractor.
  - These disruptions in your schedule could be taking a toll on you physically, leading to . . .
    - Exhaustion.
    - Strain.
    - Cantankerousness.
- So, even though you weren't injured physically, you may be affected physically.

You Have Other Reactions

- Along with disbelief, there are **other reactions** that are different from the person who was traumatized.
- These include:
  - Feeling protective toward the one who was hurt.
  - Trying to "explain" why this happened.
  - Blaming yourself and feeling guilty.
  - Feeling helpless and inadequate.
  - Feeling confused about your role in the relationship.
  - Feeling anger, which results in blaming the person traumatized.

- Feeling outraged at whomever or whatever caused the trauma.
- Feeling invisible, as if you and your needs no longer exist.
- Feeling extreme confusion if the one traumatized caused the trauma.

THE PROTECTIVE REACTION

- This is a natural response when someone you care for has been hurt.
- This reaction can often feel supportive to the one who was hurt.
- In fact, sometimes it is exactly what the person wants.
- And sometimes it is not what is wanted.
  - This is because it can make someone feel helpless, like a child and this is the very way they don't want to feel again.

> *Lynn Manning struggled to make people understand that being blind did not mean he was a baby.*[2]

- You'll need to take your cue from the person you are trying to protect.
  - If you see he or she feels supported by and grateful for your protection, keep it up!
  - If he or she seems irritated by it, this is probably a message to back off. That doesn't mean stop supporting the person, it just means stop hovering.

> *Liz took care of Sherry for quite some time after she returned home from the hospital. She stayed with her daughter as long as she could, and for most of that time Sherry was pliant and acquiescent. But then the time came to leave. How did Liz know? Liz tells me, laughing warmly, "She started getting snarly. Then it was time to leave."*[3]

🙵 The other thing about the protective reaction is that **it is often for you.** It may seem like it's for the other person, but often it is to help you take care of your fears that have been stirred up by this event. It may be to help you feel less helpless.

🙵 This is a normal reaction. When we hear about the trauma of others, we can't help but feel shaken and fearful, and feel a need for more protection. The challenge is to direct it in the right way.

THE TRYING-TO-EXPLAIN-WHY-THIS-HAPPENED REACTION

🙵 This is a common response from those close to the one hurt.

🙵 It is an effort to make some sense out of the event.

🙵 We often feel if we could just understand something and fit it into some logical explanation, then we would be more able to deal with it.

🙵 We do this because it is sometimes easier than dealing with something that is incomprehensible.

🙵 Of course, what you will find yourself hitting up against is that there is no logical explanation.

🙵 When you can't find a logical explanation, you may come up with an illogical explanation that you try to make sound logical, like "Because I decided I wanted to stay home from the basketball game, he was in an accident."

BLAMING YOURSELF AND FEELING GUILTY

- This is one of those illogical explanations that you may find yourself believing.
- Here are some examples of how it usually goes:
    - If only I hadn't had that fight with him this morning, he wouldn't have gone off by himself.
    - If only I had secured those windows the way I should have, the robber wouldn't have been able to enter the house and terrify my wife.
    - I can't seem to stop feeling guilty. I just know I could have done something to prevent this, even though I can't think of anything right now.
- All of these thoughts are efforts to make sense of the situation and to try to figure out how you could prevent it in the future—that is, how to achieve control over the situation.
- But, as stated earlier, most traumas are so unpredictable and sudden, little or nothing can be done to prevent them.

YOU MAY FEEL HELPLESS AND INADEQUATE

- You were helpless during the trauma.
- Most likely, you weren't there, so you could do nothing.
- If you were there, it is likely you were rendered helpless by some outside force.
- This state of helplessness is a difficult fact to face, but it is an irreversible fact. Just as the person who experienced the trauma, *there was nothing you could do.*
- Recognizing this fact will help you deal with the helplessness and thereby aid in understanding the helplessness of the one for whom you are caring.

> *Liz told me about her frustration because she was unable to protect her daughter. "You spend your life protecting your child. You're right beside them. And after all the time in my life I protected her, I couldn't protect her from that 'accident.' So all I could do was be a caretaker and that part was easy to do because she was very special."*[4]

You Don't Know How to Help

- Another type of helplessness that emerges after the trauma is simply a **helplessness about what to do.**
- More than likely, you desperately want to help.
- You would like to help by trying to take away what happened. It is upsetting that you can't.
- You also want to take away the pain. You cannot do that, either.
- Many things that you would like to do won't work.
- As a result, you feel inadequate.
- It is natural reaction to feeling helpless, but **being helpless is not the same as being inadequate.**

ROLE CONFUSION

❧ Many traumas lead to a **change in roles.** You will feel **confused** about this sudden role change. For example, if your wife was the one hurt, and you take over the tasks she normally performed, you will experience **role confusion.**

❧ This can be perplexing:
- You have to learn unfamiliar skills.
- You might worry that taking over someone's job might offend the person and find it difficult to discuss it with them.
- You could be overwhelmed by how much you are having to handle and be confused about the mixed feelings you're experiencing.
- If there are children, it may be difficult to explain these changes to them.
- The person you care for may have changed.

> *Shelly told me how her mother dramatically changed. "She used to be nice and sweet and so warm. She's not like that now. Her whole personality has changed. She's not warm, because she's always frustrated. Her attitude ... is so severe."*[5]

ANGER AND BLAME

🦋 You may find yourself feeling **angry,** which in turn leads to **blaming** the person who was traumatized.

  • This is common.

  • You might be embarrassed by this blaming because you feel you shouldn't feel this way.

  • But you are angry. Who wouldn't be? Your life has been disrupted. Everything is different.

  • Sometimes these feelings are an effort to deny one's vulnerability. If you can blame the person traumatized, then you can continue to deny randomness and your own vulnerability.

  • This kind of anger can also be **displacement;** that is, you become angry with someone or something other than with whom the anger really belongs.

  • In trauma, displacement onto the victim is common because often the perpetrator or the event that caused the trauma is not available to get angry with or to blame. It seems the anger has to go somewhere, so it goes to the next illogical choice, the trauma victim.

  • Uncontrolled anger and blaming can become problematic, and is something for which you should find help.

Shelly, a young mother, was struggling with taking care of her mother after her mother suffered a sudden trauma that resulted in physical disabilities. She feels her mother's frustration and anger. She also feels angry when her mother says she isn't being helpful enough. She also feels angry when her mother is being more helpless than necessary. She feels angry at how her previously independent mother has changed. She feels "angry and more angry, pretty much all the time." But, she added later, "If you love a person

> *enough, you have to understand . . . you have to*
> *have a lot of understanding because she was nor-*
> *mal a moment ago and she's not anymore." So*
> *for this young, overtaxed mother, the anger*
> *doesn't change the inalterable love for the*
> *mother who was and the mother who is.*[6]

OUTRAGE

- ☙ You may find yourself **feeling outraged at whomever or whatever caused the trauma.**
- ☙ This is very often an immediate reaction.
  - You may feel the impulse to go after the person who caused the trauma and seek revenge.
  - If a corporation was associated with the trauma (as in an air or train disaster), you may wish to go after the institution or representative associated with the company.
- ☙ To some extent, this can be a useful reaction as it is accompanied by a feeling of strength. That strength may help you take useful action—for instance, pressing charges or seeking and receiving restitution for lost wages.
- ☙ It could, however, lead to your getting involved in wasted action and in focusing your energy away from the healing process of the one for whom you care.
- ☙ The usefulness can best be measured by the degree of involvement:
  - If rage-based action takes precedence over everything else, it is probably not helpful.
  - If the action is balanced by your attending to other aspects of the aftermath of the trauma (including taking care of yourself), it is probably helpful.

INVISIBILITY

❧ You may feel **invisible.**
  - Sometimes trauma takes over everything.
  - For those of you who have children, the occurrence of a trauma is not unlike having a newborn enter the family—each pushes everything else into the background.
  - The aftereffects of the trauma often dictate everyday actions for some time.
  - This could include trips for medical help, phone calls about legal proceedings, dealing with workers rebuilding after disaster, hand holding— an infinite list of possible aftereffects that can push aside normal, everyday events.
  - *You* then feel invisible. Your needs, your exhaustion, your strain don't seem to exist. You may begin to feel like a hungry baby who wants to scream for attention, but there is no one to hear.

> *Betty felt invisible a great deal of the time. She knew that suddenly she was once again in the kind of caretaking role she had been in with each of her newborn children. Except this time she wasn't with a newborn. She was with her very grown-up husband, who was bedridden. For thirteen months, Betty was invisible. She felt she had no choice.*[7]

- You may feel invisible because the person who was traumatized may suddenly be involved with other people who have gone through the same or a similar trauma and you are left out.
- Rafael Yglesias captures this in his novel *Fearless*.[8] The two main characters, Max and Carla, were strangers before the plane crash from which they both survived. After the crash they were together, a lot. This was to the dismay and bewilderment of Max's wife, who suddenly became a backdrop to the incredible bond between Max and Carla.
- This form of invisibility is very difficult to tolerate and is difficult not to take personally. It isn't personal, though. It is only because some trauma victims have an insatiable need to be in the company of other trauma victims. It is felt that no one else can understand. And there is some truth in that.

What If the Person Traumatized Caused the Trauma?

- Sometimes it happens that the one who was traumatized caused the trauma to occur. For instance, an auto accident caused by a drunk driver or a house fire caused by a cigarette smoker.
- When this is the circumstance, it can be infuriating. You may feel intense anger toward the one you love for being so careless and having caused the trauma. The intense anger may make you feel:
  - Guilty.
  - Resentful.
  - Confused about wanting to help.
  - Doubtful about the relationship.
- In this circumstance, you may be in particular need of help in order to sort out your feelings and any decision you may need to make about the relationship and your continuing role in it. If the problem that caused the trauma (like drinking) was chronic prior to the trauma, you may want to seek out the help of such organizations as Al-Anon (a group for the loved ones of problem drinkers).

CHAPTER FIFTEEN

Helping

Deciding to Help

- Now is the time to **decide whether you will help.** It may seem odd to you that it is even suggested you have a choice about whether or not to help.
- But you do have a choice, and your decision can be extremely important to the recovery of both you and the one harmed.
- Taking care of someone you care for who has been traumatized is not mandatory.
- Those of you who have been thrown into this situation have a lot to think about, because deciding to be available to help someone through the post-trauma period is . . .
  - A big commitment.
  - Usually a relatively long commitment.
  - A decision that requires chunks of time.
  - A decision that requires sacrifices.
  - A decision that can result in exhaustion and strain, and having to put aside some of your own interests and commitments.

ᕀ Therefore, it is a decision that deserves careful consideration.

ᕀ There is a side of helping other than the responsibility side.

ᕀ This side I refer to as the **opportunity** side.

ᕀ If you decide to help, several opportunities will become apparent:

  • The chance for closeness. Most people report that their relationship to the person traumatized was strengthened by helping.

  • There is a feeling of being bonded to others in a deeper and more intense way than previously experienced.

    • In incidents of individual trauma, the bond is to the one who was hurt and to others and their loved ones who have experienced the same type of trauma.

    • In incidents of group trauma, the bond is to the community and the people within that community who have also experienced the trauma.

  • There is the opportunity to hone your ability to respond empathically to your own and another's needs.

  • There is a chance to experience the "feel good" feeling that comes from helping another person.

ᕀ In considering whether you should help, make an honest decision. That is the most helpful.

ᕀ If you can't help, then don't, because that is what will be most helpful.

ᕀ Most likely, if you are close to the person traumatized, you will help. This is usually what we do when we care for someone who is hurt.

What Will Help You

~ If you have decided to help, there are certain helpful ways to approach being a helper.

~ Try to think about the extent to which you can help.

- Think about the best hours for you to be available.
- Think about what types of help you are most comfortable providing. For example,
  - Errands.
  - Listening.
  - Transportation.
  - Phone calls.
- While thinking about the extent to which you can help, keep in mind . . .
  - You can only do what you can do.
  - Whatever you do is good enough (and may often feel like not enough).
  - You have limits because you are human.
  - To do more than you comfortably can is unfair to you and to the one you are helping.

YOUR REACTIONS

~ You are trying to help under extraordinary conditions, which means you may have **extraordinary reactions.** You may . . .

- Anger more easily.
- Tire more easily.
- Become depressed more easily.
- Become frustrated more easily.
- Feel resentful.
- Wish you could jump ship.

🏕 All of these feelings are to be expected. They are not a blemish on your character or on your wish to help.

🏕 It is most helpful if you can make allowances for yourself and for these feelings. They are all within the range of what is normal given your circumstances.

🏕 It is also helpful to **have your own helpers**—people to whom you can go who can listen to your problems. Remember, the one traumatized is not the only one upset and, therefore, is not the only one who needs a sympathetic ear.

AVOIDING BURNOUT

🏕 "Quit while you are ahead."
  • This is an old truth that fits well in this situation.
  • Let yourself take breaks.
  • Let yourself back out of a commitment if you need a break.
  • Try to think ahead so you don't offer to do more than you can.
  • Get support from others.
  • **Let yourself be selfish.**
  • Keep in mind that you cannot take care of anyone else if you first don't take care of yourself.
  • Take care of yourself physically by . . .
    • Eating well.
    • Resting.
    • Exercising.
  • This is the best preventive for avoiding burnout.

What Will Not *Help You*

- **Don't mistakingly believe you can do more than you can.**
  - You are just a regular person, no matter how much you may wish otherwise.
  - Do not overdose on caretaking.
- **Stay away from nonsupporters.**
  - This is as important for you as it is for the one who was hurt.
  - Nonsupporters usually are . . .
    - Critical.
    - Insensitive.
    - Judgmental.
    - Righteous.
    - Impatient.
  - They are not good for you. You need . . .
    - Acceptance.
    - Sensitivity.
    - Understanding.
    - Compassion.
    - Patience.
- **Don't minimize your emotions.**
  - Do not deny or hide your feelings from yourself about the trauma, because it will lead to . . .
    - Resentment.
    - Frustration.
    - Dishonesty followed by loss of trust.
    - Burnout.
    - Isolation.
- **Avoid survivor guilt.**
  - Your suffering will not take away what occurred.
    - If it is excessive, you should find help, because it will interfere with what needs to be done.
- **Don't slip into isolation.** We all need to refuel and we need others to help.
  - Avoid the trap of isolation.
  - You'll burn out sooner if you don't have your own source of support.

What Will Help the One You Are Helping

- Very often what a traumatized person needs the most is **sensitive ears,** so make yourself available for listening.
- Some people need to hear that you would like to listen because they worry they will be bothersome to you.
    - A simple comment like, "Anytime you want to talk about what happened, I am here to listen" will probably be enough.
- Many traumatized people need to repeat their story over and over.
    - This is part of healing.
    - Therefore, you need to be ready to hear it over and over.
    - This need will diminish over time (a sign of recovery).
    - If it does not, then professional help may be indicated.
- You can also let the person know that you not only want to listen, but that in order to help, you need to know what he or she is going through and what is needed from you. This **invitation to talk** will be welcomed by most.

LISTENING

- **There is a way to listen.**
  - To understand how to listen, think of the response you would want if you were on the other end.
  - You don't have to do much more than listen.
  - Just listening, along with simple comments like, "I can see why you feel that way" or "That must be hard" is usually all that is necessary.
- Behave toward the traumatized person the way a **compassionate parent** would behave toward a child.
- An attitude of compassion will help the person feel understood.
- And just as a hurt child needs compassion, the traumatized adult needs **reassurance.**
  - A traumatized person's sense of safety has been disrupted. The world doesn't feel safe.
  - The person needs to hear, over and over, that it's going to be okay.
  - He or she also needs to hear that there are ways to make it okay (realistic ways, that is).
- Here is where **information** is helpful. For instance, it would be helpful to know what the odds are that this could happen again and what safety measures are available to minimize future occurrences and negative outcomes.

OFFERING PRACTICAL HELP

- There is one last way you can help.
- Find out what the person needs in terms of **practical help.**
  - Are there errands to run?
  - Is transportation needed?
  - Is help needed to make phone calls?
  - Should food be provided?
  - Are there safety devices to be installed?
  - Does something require rebuilding and repairing?
- This type of practical assistance can be a tremendous support. If this is where you shine, this is what you should do.

What Will Not Help the One You Are Helping

- 🔊 The overriding don't in helping someone is **don't cut off communication.**
- 🔊 There are certain ways communication is cut off:
    - **By making it obvious you are not available to listen,** for example, by changing the topic when the person tries to talk about the trauma.
    - **By blaming the person,** in any way, for what occurred—for example, "Well, if you hadn't carried all that cash with you . . ." or "You should never have been walking in that area by yourself" or "You should never have moved to where they have tornadoes."
    - **By minimizing what the person is feeling**—for example, "Oh, it wasn't that bad" or "I just can't understand why you are so upset; you only lost your purse when you were mugged."
    - **By suggesting the trauma shouldn't be talked about**—for example, "You should just forget that—it's over now" or "If you just keep talking about it, it will make it worse."
    - **By minimizing the loss**—for example, "Well, it could have been worse" or "At least you weren't hurt."
        - Just because the hurt doesn't show does not mean it's not there.
        - **Most of life's worst hurts can't be seen.**
    - **By suggesting it was fate**—for example, "It was probably meant to happen."
    - **By being critical of the person's type of expression**—for example, "I just don't understand why you're crying about this."
        - There is no right way to express upset. Everyone does it his or her own way.
    - **By telling the person you know "exactly" how they feel.**

- You may not know.
- If you had a similar experience, you could say how you felt and inquire if the person is feeling the same. This gives the person a chance to say how he or she is feeling.

- Overall, the kinds of comments listed here will guarantee the end of any attempt to communicate, which will interfere with recovery.
- If you cannot communicate effectively, back away and let someone else be the listener.
- If you've had trouble communicating, but after reading this think you can do it differently, try again. Someone who has been traumatized will respond quickly and positively to someone who is trying, even if that person didn't do so well before.

WHEN NOT TO INTERFERE

& **Don't tell the person what he or she should or should not do.**

- Traumatized people usually have a good sense of what will help them.
- Their decisions may seem silly, stupid, outrageous, impractical, and/or ridiculous to you. Let them do it anyway.
- For instance if . . .
  - A hurricane survivor wants to buy a marine radio to have more accurate and immediate weather information, don't argue.
  - A burglary victim wants to put triple locks on every door and window, along with installing a high tech alarm system, don't argue.
  - A carjacking victim wants to drive an old, beat-up car from now on, don't argue.
- People who have been traumatized know what they need to do to make themselves feel safe.
- The action they want to take may be the last one you would take or even would think of taking.
- That doesn't make it wrong. It just makes it different.

WHEN TO INTERFERE

- ☙ If you find yourself starting to object to the person's decisions, remember that these sorts of actions heal.
- ☙ They give the traumatized person a feeling he or she can do something to provide safety and to overcome helplessness.
- ☙ **Of course, there are always exceptions.** The time to interfere with an action is:
  - When it looks like it could put the person in danger.
  - When you are worried the person is using extremely poor judgment.
  - If the person is trying to make a really big decision that could have a major effect on their future or their family's or partner's.
    - Obviously, buying a marine radio doesn't require interference, whereas deciding to move out of the area right after the trauma might.
- ☙ In the case of an extreme action or decision, encourage more thought before the action is taken.

> *Dede quit one job and took another five days after the Northridge, California, earthquake. She worked at the new job for four days and realized she had made a big mistake. It had been an impulsive decision during a time when she was too emotionally upset to think through what was best for her. It would have been helpful to have someone slow her down and encourage her to give the decision some time.*[1]

PART SIX

Traumatized Children

Ah! What would the world be to us
If the children were no more?
We should dread the desert behind us
Worse than the dark before.[1]

CHAPTER SIXTEEN

Common Questions

Ila and I spoke via long distance, Los Angeles to Miami. Earthquake country to hurricane country. Connection.

Ila lives in a U-shaped house. Half the bedrooms are on one wing, the other half on the other. The kitchen, great room, and foyer are in between. The night the hurricane was threatening, Ila went with her youngest son into the master bedroom. She thought this room would be safe because it had no windows. The noise from the storm, however, kept waking her son and as a result, she took him into his room to lie down. Ila's parents were in the house that night as well. They came to Ila for shelter because their home was in an area that had to be evacuated. They were in another room on the same wing of the house. Her husband and oldest son were in the other wing along with another family who had also been evacuated. As she rested with her son, Ila said the noise from the storm became increasingly loud, each new noise more remarkable than the one before. She found it hard to describe, but said it was something like the noise from an airport runway.

Suddenly, she heard a crash followed by the smell of fresh-cut grass. She felt a wave of panic, imagining what had happened to let the storm come into the house. She grabbed Ryan and went to alert her parents. As she was running down the corridor, she could sense that the wind was in the house. With Ryan clutching her like a baby monkey, she told her parents to put on their shoes and follow her. Her intention was to have all of them go to the other wing. As they approached the connecting foyer, she saw her husband approaching from the other side of the house. He called out to her and told her the front doors had blown open and to go back to the other wing. She led her group back to her son's room, thinking it would be a safe place because of the way the window had been constructed. But that very window was shaking and it frightened her, so she led them all back out again, thinking that if the front doors had been shut they could safely cross to the other side. Foliage and trees were now flying into the house. Ila's husband saw her attempting to cross over and waved her back, screaming over the sound of the storm to take cover. Ila now had no choice but to remain in her son's room. Ryan was clutching her so tightly she did not even have to use her arms to hold him to her. She used her arms, instead, to pull apart her son's car bed. She put the mattress against the door and the bed against the mattress and then lay down on the floor with her parents and her son to wait in frozen terror.

Ila doesn't know how long it all lasted. She does know that she was speechless, that her immovable son spent the rest of the night on top of her, that her mother prayed to every relative who had passed away, and that her usually macho father, a veteran of Florida storms, couldn't even muster a face of bravado. Andrew was different from any other storm and from any other experience.

The light of day reunited the family. There was mud, dirt, water, foliage, and tree roots along with pieces of other houses in their living area. But that was all right, for they knew that what was important was each other and that they were safe and together. They were grateful.

It took a few days to realize that although everyone was all right physically, something had happened to the way they were with each other. It seemed their personalities had changed. Some of those changes turned out to be temporary, while others appear to be permanent.

Ila's oldest son, Jerrod, who was four when Andrew hit, became more demanding than the typical four-year-old. He became mean and aggressive, striking out at his younger brother and having tantrums if he didn't get his way. He would become so distraught and disruptive that on some occasions, when they were in public places, Ila would have to carry him out. And because she was so upset herself, it would sometimes escalate into her yelling and screaming. She had lost the ability to sit back and think and control herself. She had lost the ability to count to 10.

She would apologize to Jerrod and explain, "Mommy is a little crazy right now. We've been through a lot, we don't have our own house to go to, and I'm sorry about getting upset with you, but everything scares me, too."

Ryan, the clinging monkey child, was two years old when Andrew came. Ryan and his mother used to sit outside on the patio when it rained. They liked doing that together. Ryan doesn't like the rain anymore. He jumps and becomes terrified when he hears the rain and thunder. He won't sleep in his own room when *there is rain. Ila's anxiety level also increases when she hears the rain and she likes nothing about it anymore.*

Some things are better now. Jerrod's aggressiveness has diminished. Ryan is somewhat less frightened at the sound of storms, although he still won't sleep alone. But Ila feels she has changed, that she has lost something—something more essential to her than just enjoying rain. Ila had lived a good life, one she felt she had control over. But when Hurricane Andrew came, for the first time she feared for her life and, worse, she feared for her children's lives. She felt a responsibility for them. They were terrified and there was nothing she could do about it. Ila and her children used to have a saying. It goes like this:

ILA: *A MOM*

JERROD AND RYAN: . . . *can do anything!!*

This time Mom couldn't do anything. As she said, "I couldn't save them from the storm. I couldn't make it go away, I couldn't prevent them from going through it. . . . Even though I was there, their world was not safe. I don't know if they feel [that they were unprotected], but I do. I'm different now because something was taken away and I don't know if I'm going to get it back."[1]

First Comments

- ☛ If your child was traumatized, you may be . . .
  - Wishing, more than anything, that it hadn't happened.
  - Hoping that it won't affect your child.
  - Hoping to find ways to undo what happened.
  - Wondering how it might affect your child.
- ☛ You also may be . . .
  - Finding yourself in a state of shock and disbelief that this could have happened to your child.
  - Feeling a deep sense of responsibility along with the belief you should have been able to prevent it.
  - Feeling outrage, especially if it was a person who hurt your child.
  - Feeling helpless.
  - Wondering what you should do now.

The First Question

- 🍋 **Do traumatic events affect children?**
  - **Yes.**
  - There is no doubt that trauma affects children.
  - It is understandable if you were hoping for a different answer.
  - However, there have been many studies of children who have experienced trauma, and **no matter what age they are,** they were affected.[2]
  - Not all children are affected in the same way, but there are some recognizable and predictable effects.

"For three days [my daughter] relived the trauma in her sleep. From her screams and what she said, we knew she was reliving moments at the crash site or in the hospital. When my husband tried to comfort her, she did not recognize him. She thought he was the paramedic or the doctor . . . and screamed hysterically."[3]

NOTE: This book is for adults and children who have experienced a *one-time* trauma. Children who have been traumatized repetitively will show different reactions, and this book should not be considered a resource for those situations.

The Second Question

❧ Why does trauma affect children?

- Children who are being raised in a stable environment experience the world as ordered and safe. This is what helps children grow and become whole.
- However, trauma is not an experience of orderliness or safety.
- Instead, trauma brings chaos and insecurity.
- Children are in the process of becoming whole. The puzzle that represents a child has some fuzzy borders that haven't yet been completed and a lot of the inside pieces haven't yet been put into place.
- Open borders leave more openings for the trauma to affect the inside. This can throw the existing pieces into greater disarray.
- Finally, children are already helpless in many ways.
  - They are still growing toward independence and autonomy.
  - They are small and feel small.
  - The trauma intensifies that feeling.
  - The feelings of smallness coupled with helplessness bring feelings of shame.
  - They are unable to think about the trauma in a way that grown-ups can; therefore, it is harder for them to understand and give meaning to the trauma.

A little girl told her psychiatrist, "I am ashamed ... it makes me feel smaller than a person."[4]

The Third Question

ક• **Will your child remember the trauma?**
- **YES.**
- There is a myth that children do not remember what happened when they were young.
- This is generally not true.
- The exceptions are cases of long-term trauma, such as being kidnapped for a long time or being repeatedly sexually abused. In these situations, the experience may be out of consciousness, sometimes for years, sometimes forever.
- But the kind of trauma discussed here (a one-time trauma) is remembered.
- In fact, it is remembered with remarkable accuracy.
  - Children who are verbal and not too afraid or ashamed will be able to tell about the event in vivid detail.
  - Children who are still preverbal will show the details of the trauma in their play or behavior, or through bodily experience.

The Fourth Question

- **Will your child deny the trauma?**
    - More than likely, **no,** unless they were threatened.
    - **But you may.**
    - Many parents try to deny that . . .
        - The trauma happened.
        - The trauma will affect their child.
        - Their child will remember the trauma.
    - This is often because the parents are overwhelmed by the painful fact that their child was hurt.
    - Sometimes it is harder to bear than if it had happened to you.

"Her father and I had to endure this helplessly. Some residue of that horror will always remain. Even if I exorcise it mentally, a portion of that agony is lodged in my body. It can never be removed."[5]

- As you will see in Chapter 18, it is very important that you try not to deny the trauma and the impact it has had on your child.
- This will help your child deal more easily with what has happened. Try to keep in mind that just because your child looks okay (if your child wasn't physically injured), it does not necessarily mean your child is okay.

CHAPTER SEVENTEEN

Children's Reactions

- ❧ Many children **regress**.
- ❧ This means that your child may start behaving like a younger child.
- ❧ For instance, children who were potty-trained may start wetting the bed.
- ❧ Regression is an attempt to return to a time when the child felt safer—a time *before* the trauma.
- ❧ *Regression is very common.*
- ❧ You need not worry about it unless it lasts for a long while.
- ❧ If it does last, it is a message that your child hasn't recovered and needs additional help.

NOTE: Children are more likely to tell us about their upsets through their behavior than through their words. This is true even when they are verbal. You can learn a lot about what your child is experiencing by noting changes in behavior, including play.

General Reactions

HYPERAROUSAL

- Children may show signs of **hyperarousal**.
- This may be seen in:
  - Nightmares.
  - Physical complaints.
  - Being easily startled.
  - "Psychophysiologic reenactments."[1]
    - Lenore Terr, an expert in childhood trauma, coined this phrase to describe how traumatized children reenact the traumatic experience through reexperiencing certain feelings in their bodies that were experienced at the time of the trauma.

Five children from the Chowchilla bus kidnapping incident had bladder problems four years following the trauma. None of these five had a physical basis for the problem. The bladder problems mimicked the experience during the kidnapping when, without a bathroom, there was an urgency to urinate, a need to withhold urine, and a loss of urine.[2]

PERSONALITY CHANGES

- Some children may show **personality changes.**
- One of the most dramatic personality changes and one of the most upsetting to grown-ups is when a child becomes assaultive and aggressive. Traumas by their nature are assaultive and children who have been traumatized are sometimes vulnerable to identifying themselves with the assaultiveness or aggressiveness of the occurrence and/or person that caused the trauma. This defense mechanism is called "identification with the aggressor" and children do this in order to feel powerful rather than helpless. It can cause children remarkable personality changes. A mild-mannered child can become irritable, angry, aggressive, and explosive.

> *A sister, once a sweet and gentle child, now swears at her family, dresses in men's clothes, and brandishes a toy machine gun.*[3]

- Other examples of changes are:
  - A formerly independent child may cling and not be willing to try to do things independent of help or company.
  - A child who was a good student may begin to have failing grades.
  - A social child may become withdrawn and isolated.
  - A cooperative child may become belligerent and undisciplined.
  - A happy child may become depressed and sad.

> *"Cataline Martinez's ten-year-old daughter bravely guided her three young siblings out of danger when fire and smoke engulfed their second-floor apartment.... These days [she] suffers from severe melancholy. 'She was always very happy. Now, she's very sad. She's not the way she used to be.' "*[4]

❧ Children who show these kinds of changes need professional help because:
  - Such dramatic changes are a sign the child is very upset.
  - These actions are a cry for help.
  - Without help, these changes could become a permanent part of their personality.

FEARS

❧ Your child is very likely to have **fears**.
❧ Your child's fears may be very specific to the trauma.
  - For instance, a child traumatized by a flood may be fearful of the sound of moving water.

> *This is the case for Greg's daughter. Since the flood of 1993, she can no longer sleep in the lower level of the house when it rains.*[5]

❧ Dr. Lenore Terr also identified "fears of the mundane" as an outcome of trauma in children.[6]
  - These include such things as fears of the dark, fears of strangers, and even fears of previously enjoyed television programs or bedtime stories.
❧ These fears of the mundane may be the same as normal childhood fears, except that they are more intense and long-lasting and usually they cause panic. That is how you know they are trauma-related.
❧ If these fears were traced to where they began, they would be found to have something to do with the trauma.
❧ These fears can cause a child to never really feel safe.

Rigidity

🙪 A common reaction of traumatized children is **rigidity.**

- The face of a traumatized child was captured by Steven Spielberg in the movie *Jurassic Park*. The faces of the two children in the movie were studies of the rigidified horror that often accompanies trauma.
- This rigidity occurs during the actual trauma, but unfortunately it often remains.
- Children who were able to adjust to new situations pre-trauma can no longer do so. For instance, instead of going outdoors, they may only want to stay home where everything is familiar.
- Their behavior replicates the mask that formed on their faces at the time of the trauma, that is, they may be quiet and withdrawn and feel unable to play and imagine.
- They attempt to deal with the trauma by living lives of constriction rather than amplification.
- They do this out of the fear of reexperiencing fear.
- This may keep them from blossoming.

If the rigidity is not resolved, it will show up in adulthood. You will see a colorlessness, a deadness, a lack of imagination, an inability to play. I have had the opportunity to work with a man who deadened himself many years ago because of a sudden and shocking trauma that happened when he was seven. There is a boy in him, somewhere, a boy who played, who knew how to have fun. Once in a while the boy shows up and we discover a delightful, pre-trauma child, a child gleaming with warmth and mirth, a child who isn't afraid. When he blossoms, he fears. He doesn't think so, but I know so because I see him go away and then I wait, sometimes for a long time, for him to try, once again, to come out and play.[7]

EFFECTS ON PLAY

🞲 Trauma has **an effect on play.**
- Play is one of the main ways children express themselves. Play is usually imaginative and creative and changeable. It flourishes. And within it, children can be who they want, what they want, and where they want.
- This may be lost for traumatized children.
- The play of traumatized children is often the same, over and over.
  - It is monotonous.
  - It is rigid.
  - It is realistic.
  - It is the trauma, often with little disguise.
  - They can't help but play this way. There is little choice.
  - The trauma may be repeated in this fashion until it is resolved.

Mary talks about her son's play following Hurricane Andrew. "He was playing with his friends. They had made a little fort out of the table. They put a sheet over it. He started running around the table saying, 'The storm is coming, the storm is coming.'"[8]

THE QUESTION OF A FUTURE

- ❧ Usually, we spend many, many years believing in our invincibility.
- ❧ Some people spend a lifetime believing they will live forever and nothing bad will befall them.
- ❧ Often, children who have been traumatized lose this sense of invincibility.
- ❧ They know they can die.
- ❧ And some children, because they know they can die, **don't believe they have a future.**
- ❧ Often, they have the belief they will die at a certain age.
- ❧ Usually, this is a much younger age than would normally be expected.

> *"I already know what it's like to die—to be killed. You feel real scared, can't breathe," said Alan, an eight-year-old kidnap victim, to Dr. Terr.*[9]

- ❧ And because they believe they will die, they don't have plans and they don't make plans.
- ❧ They are sure their future will bring calamity. Absolutely sure. They are just waiting.
- ❧ They have seen too much. They know it can happen.

> *Most people with whom I work have this sense of futurelessness and impending calamity. They are shocked to hear that it isn't this way for everyone. For them, it is a given. They are saddened when they realize other people have future dreams and they have none, that they don't even know how to dream. Why have dreams when at any moment disaster will strike?*
>
> *Lynn Manning figured something awful might happen to him and it did. He was shot, which caused the loss of his sight.*

> *After we had talked about all of that, I asked*
> *Lynn if he still had that feeling that something*
> *would happen to him. His answer? "Well, I*
> *don't actually. In that same way I don't, but*
> *there's this one little thing that irks me a little*
> *bit. There was this idea when I was thirteen that*
> *I wouldn't make it past forty-five. I don't place*
> *any value in the premonition thing, but I'll worry*
> *about it when forty-five approaches."*
> *Lynn's boyhood was surrounded by trauma.*
> *He saw people die. He saw a foreshortened fu-*
> *ture.*[10]

IGNORING AND REMEMBERING

- Children don't forget the trauma, but they try to ignore it.
- They try to ignore it, mostly, because they are ashamed.
- It makes them feel smaller and more helpless, which they don't want to feel.

> *Dr. Terr speaks of how much the Chowchilla*
> *kidnap children hated "The Rock," a monument*
> *that was erected in their town by the adults in*
> *gratitude for the children being returned. They*
> *did not want this visible sign of their shame and*
> *helplessness—they hated it and what it repre-*
> *sented.*[11]

- Children don't seem to have intrusive recollections or flashbacks in which they feel they are right back in the event.
- Instead, they see the experience as it floats in and out of their normal course of thinking.
- These memories are not welcome or voluntary.
- Most children do not find these memories occurring during periods of concentration, but more often during periods of daydreaming.

- For most children it doesn't interfere with their school-work. However, some can be distracted, and in their effort to ignore what happened to them, they ignore everything else.
- The age of a child and the level of maturity and accomplishment lead to different reactions to trauma.
- It is helpful to think about where children are in their development in order to understand their behavior.
- Knowing where your child is developmentally is critical to determining if your child is showing signs of regression and, therefore, trauma.
- On the following pages, possible outcomes following trauma are listed for specific age groups.[12]
- If you have questions about your child's level of development, you may want to consult with your child's teacher. Also, it is essential to inform your child's teacher about the trauma so that the teacher understands any changes in your child and can aid in your child's recovery.

Birth to Age Six

- Babies and small children almost always have only their behavior to signal their distress. There are no or few words.
- Infants may show more irritability, crying, and a need to be held more often and for longer periods of time.
- There are nighttime terrors, including fear of going to sleep, having bad dreams, fear of the dark, etc.
- Small children may be more dependent until they can once again feel safe, trusting, and secure.
- A lack of security may lead your child to be unable to explore the world as before.
- If there has been loss and separation of any kind, your child may be afraid of being abandoned. Grown-ups are everything to children, and the dependency of children is absolute. Therefore, the loss or threatened loss of the grown-ups in their world is terrifying to children.

- The lack of security and fear of abandonment can result in anxiety that can show up in irritability, unusual outbursts, and general out-of-control behavior.
- Or it can also show up in the opposite. A quieting of behavior where withdrawal, mutism, and rigidity are used to bind anxiety.
- Some children express their distress through their bodies, through physical rather than behavioral signs.

There was a child whose family apartment went up in flames. She now suffers from mysterious high fevers that have no physical basis, a painfully exquisite physical metaphor for having been the near fatal victim of a fire.[13]

- Some small children purposefully hurt themselves or their siblings or their dolls or their pets. Often this is a behavioral reenactment of the trauma that includes an attempt to show what happened to them. It is also a cry for help.

Ages Six to Twelve

- Children in this age range might also show signs of regressing—that is, behaving younger than they are.
- Some show a decline in school, but others may not. Their behavior will depend on the nature of the trauma, their support system, whether their sleep has been interrupted, and whether they are depressed.
- Your child may be talking repeatedly about the trauma. This initially may be an attempt to master the trauma; however, if it lasts for more than a few weeks or months it may indicate difficulty mastering the trauma.
- Children in this group may feel a sense of guilt and failure resulting from the belief that they should have been more heroic. They may also be engaging in fantasies of revenge that might be apparent in their play.

- They may be angry at those whom they feel should have protected them or angry at themselves for being vulnerable.

- They may be fearful of places, things and/or people. They will avoid these things in order not to feel fear.

- They may be fearful of abandonment, especially if they were threatened with actual separation or loss.

> *Mary, a traffic cop who was hit by a car, had a teenage daughter at the time of the incident. Mary's daughter felt fearful that her mother, who was her only parent, would be lost to her through death. And because of that fear, she reacted, behaving in more extreme ways than normal, even for a teenager.*[14]

- In order to counteract their fears, some children may take chances as they try to prove themselves invulnerable.

- There may be physical complaints, like stomachaches or headaches.

- They may be more competitive with siblings, especially a younger sibling.

- Death, their own and that of loved ones, may be on their mind.

- They may be particularly on guard and alert to noises, to sudden changes, to strange people, like hyperarousal in adults.

Teenagers

- Teens know how trauma can affect their lives. They, unlike younger children, have more ability to think about how it can affect them.
- Often, because of the trauma, teens no longer feel invulnerable. This is the opposite of what teens commonly feel.
- They may levy harsh judgments against themselves regarding their behavior during the trauma, believing they should have done more.
- They can regress and act younger than they are.
- They may become antisocial. They may withdraw from normal activities and resort to acting-out behaviors like substance abuse, indiscriminate sex, or criminal activity.
- They may try to push themselves into becoming more adultlike in order to feel more grown-up and in control or in order to care for the grown-ups around them, who they perceive are floundering or damaged or hurt because of the trauma.
- As with all ages, sleep disorders and other types of hyperarousal are possible.
- Suicide is more possible for this age group.
- You may see depression, isolation, and withdrawal from friends and activities.
- Some may feel immune because they survived. The danger may be involving themselves in risky behaviors such as reckless driving. This is called counterphobic behavior, which is defined as doing that which one is afraid of in order to counteract the fear.
- The trauma may delay the striving for independence, usually seen during the teen years.

CHAPTER EIGHTEEN

What to Do

In the Aftermath of the Trauma

- Parents and/or grown-ups can make all the difference in a child's recovery from the trauma. As stated earlier, a child will be traumatized when exposed to trauma. But if children are given the proper support they can process the trauma much more quickly than most grown-ups and, therefore, bounce back more easily.
- Because a child's recovery is so dependent on the reaction of the grown-ups in their world, it creates a lot of pressure to do the right thing.
- If you, the caregiver, were also involved in the trauma, you will be under enormous pressure . . .
    - To care for yourself and your reactions to the trauma.
    - To care for your children and their reactions to the trauma.
- You must first assess your capability in being the primary caretaker.
- If you conclude you can't be the main caretaker, find someone, like a friend or relative, who can.
- That way, you can have what you need to recover and your child can as well.
- Children's recovery is dependent on their parents' recovery, so you must take care of yourself first.

STAYING TOGETHER

- The most important need your child has is to **stay with the family,** if at all possible.
- Sometimes the natural reaction is to send children to grandma's or a friend's house following a trauma.
- Unfortunately, being sent elsewhere can sometimes further traumatize children.
- Children often feel abandoned during this type of separation.
- They may interpret being sent away to mean they were bad and are being punished.
- Also, children often imagine the worst if they can't see you and be reassured by your presence.
- They worry they may never see you again or that the trauma could reoccur and they would be alone and unable to find you.
- Separation from parents, under the best of circumstances, is difficult for children. Under traumatic circumstances, it can be terrifying.
- Tell your children that the family will stay together, and take steps to ensure that. This will have an immediate positive effect.
- However, if you or your spouse also experienced the trauma, it may be impossible to keep your child with you. There are circumstances when this may occur. If this is your circumstance, place your child with someone you trust and, preferably, someone they know. Stay in as much contact as possible, via visits or telephone or letter. This will help offset some of the potentially difficult effects of a separation at this time.

ROUTINE

- ❧ The second important need your child has is **routine.**
  - Trauma equals chaos.
  - Routine equals order.
- ❧ Organize your child's post-trauma experience by introducing order as soon as possible.
- ❧ This can be done in simple ways:
  - Regulate bedtime.
  - Regulate mealtime.
  - Assign age-appropriate chores.
  - Return your child to school as soon as possible.
  - Create a special time of day (fifteen minutes is enough) just for you and your child to . . .
    - Read.
    - Talk.
    - Play.
    - Hold.
  - Be consistent. Consistency is a mainstay for children. They feel safe if they know they can rely on their world remaining the same.

INFORMATION

- ❧ The third important need your child has is to be given **information.**
- ❧ Many times adults worry that children are better off not knowing.
- ❧ But it does help them to know.
  - Give your child age-specific information.
  - Tell your child what the plan is for taking care of the trauma. For example, explain the . . .
    - Plans to clean up and rebuild.
    - Plans to go for medical and/or psychological treatment.
    - Plans for future prevention.
  - Talk to your child about how people feel after a trauma, including your feelings and his or hers.
  - The rule of thumb is, **don't keep your child in the dark.** It will only frighten your child further.

GUIDANCE AND REASSURANCE

🙦 The fourth important need your child has is for you **to be in control, to guide, and to reassure.**

🙦 If you are showing signs of stress, so will your child. This does not mean that you should deny you are upset. It only means not to overburden or overwhelm your child with your worries and stresses.

🙦 Your child's greatest fears will be that the trauma will happen again, and if it does it will result in separation and abandonment.

🙦 **Reassure** your child that you will all stay together, that it is unlikely another trauma will occur, and that the family is going to prepare for any future occurrence.

🙦 **Guidance is reassurance in the form of information.**

TALKING

🙦 The fifth important need your child has is **to talk.**

🙦 In order to talk, your child will need to sense that you can and will listen.

🙦 He or she will need to know you will listen with sensitivity and without judgment.

- Little children may try to "talk" by showing you through play or behavior. This kind of talk is harder to listen to, but not impossible. For instance, if your children are fretful, they are telling you they need something more, perhaps reassurance, perhaps just being held.

- If you have more than one child, each child may be trying to express himself differently. Listen to them talking to each other and watch their play. There will be many clues about what they have to say about the trauma in their conversations with each other and in their play.

- Invite talking about the trauma. You could open by saying, "I was thinking about (the accident or the bad man who hurt you or the flood) a minute ago. I wonder if you think about it?"
- Set aside a special time for talking and think of including the whole family. When one person can talk about his or her feelings, it often helps others to talk.
- Many children talk through drawing. You may want to introduce this by having available drawing materials and then talking with your children about what they have drawn.

A FEW MORE TIDBITS

- If you have little children, you may need to prepare yourself to allow your child some regression.
  - For instance, if your child wants a bottle after not having one for a year, give it to your child.
- Allowing regression, however, does not mean becoming inconsistent. So if you are going to allow the bottle, do it consistently and remember to maintain rules around other routines. Most children will give up the regressive behavior on their own.
- If your children are big enough to help, involve them in post-trauma activities. It will help them feel in control and feel useful.

> *Living near the worst of the Los Angeles riots was very traumatizing for a psychologist and his family. The whole family went to help at the First AME Church in South Central Los Angeles. He said it was especially helpful because they could see that others were more traumatized than they were, helping them keep their own trauma in perspective.*[1]

- If you have teens, involve them in post-trauma activities. If it's a community disaster, most teens will feel great about pitching in and helping.
- Try to keep your teens in whatever activities they were engaged in prior to the trauma.
- Remind a child of any age that it is normal to feel scared, disrupted, and confused following a trauma. It will help him or her know that you feel that, too.

Preparation for Future Trauma

- Perhaps it seems odd that I include a discussion of preparing your child for future trauma.
- For some people, it brings up concerns that it might frighten children unnecessarily to think about what could happen in the future.
- There could be reason to be concerned if discussions about future traumas were presented in a frightening way.
- But if you present it matter of factly, it will not frighten children. Instead, it will reassure them because . . .
    - With proper information it will put trauma in perspective—yes, trauma happens, but not that often.
    - It will let them know they can be prepared.
    - Having them know they can prepare helps them feel in control.
    - Knowing they have some control helps a child feel less helpless.
    - It **gives them something to do now,** which helps them cope with the current trauma.

EXPLANATIONS

- Tell your child that traumas do happen, but that they happen a zillion times less often than the regular happenings in life.
- Tell your child that traumas are something we cannot control, but . . .
  - You *can* control how you react to them after they happen.
  - You *can* control how you prepare for them before they happen.
- Tell your child that almost everyone experiences trauma —friends, family, old people, young people, pets, preachers, wild animals, teachers, doctors, and rock stars.
- Tell them that you are going to teach them how to protect themselves as much as possible *and* you are going to teach them how to react to an emergency.

INFORMATION

- The following are the essentials for your child to know for any type of trauma. Your child should **memorize all vital information.**
  - Emergency 911 and its correct use.
  - Telephone numbers of parents and other extended family or friends both in the area and out of state, at work and at home.
  - Home address.
  - Addresses of designated meeting places, if home is unreachable.
  - Routes to and from school and to and from a pre-established emergency meeting place.
- For children who are too young, put the basic information on a small card and figure out a fun place for the child to keep it when away from home—for example, in a shoe—and when at home—for example, in the cookie jar.

PLANS

- ❧ **Develop a plan** that includes the whole family.
  - If your child is old enough, have your child call the Red Cross or other organizations and request information on how to plan for emergencies.
  - If you live in an area where there is potential for a particular kind of trauma, the Red Cross usually publishes something about that. For instance, in California they have information specific to earthquake preparation.
  - Have your child ask for that specific information and any general information on how to prepare for emergencies.
  - If your child is too young to call, then you can do it but have your child listen while you make the call so he or she can learn how to ask for the information.
  - Once you have received the information, have the family meet to take the steps for good emergency planning.
- ❧ You will probably need to plan more than one meeting to cover everything and to practice.
- ❧ Yes, that's right, practice! It can be very helpful to your child to have a run-through of what to do in case of an emergency, and it can be fun for the whole family.

ADDITIONAL TIPS

- ❧ While the Red Cross provides guidelines for emergencies like fires and natural disasters, you may need to go to other resources to prepare for traumas that are caused by humans, such as robberies or assaults or auto accidents.
- ❧ Remember to be **matter of fact.** The idea is not to frighten your child, but to prepare your child. A calm manner will communicate a matter-of-fact attitude.

❧ Do not do all of this at once.

- Consider informing your child of emergency preparation as just another part of parenting your child.
- Do it in stages, remembering that in the post-trauma stage the most important message to get across is that **you are in control** and that your child can be in control by being a part of emergency planning.

PART SEVEN

When Someone

Dies

---

*Life belongs to the living, and he who lives
must be prepared for changes.*[1]

CHAPTER NINETEEN

When an Adult Loses Someone

There is so much you don't know when you are only sixteen.

Richard and his best friend, Chuck, were traveling to Bishop, California. Because it was August, it was well over 100 degrees. They had a third passenger—a dog belonging to Richard's mother. The heat caused the dog to be sick inside the Jeep and the odor made Richard and Chuck feel ill. They stopped alongside the road to clean up the mess. After driving along a bit longer, they realized it didn't work and there was still another forty miles to go with the unbearable odor. Then they had the brainstorm to spray the interior with cologne and aerosol deodorant. It brought some relief, at least for a few miles, until Chuck began to complain of feeling sick again. Richard told him to let him know if he needed to pull over, while at the same time thinking to himself that he did not feel well, either. That was the last earthly thought Richard remembered until he woke up strapped down in an ambulance with five men in white telling him not to move. They told him he had been in an accident and was seriously injured. Richard glanced down at his body and saw that he was covered with blood. Someone told him Chuck was all right and was being taken to another hospital.

It was assumed that, because of his age, Richard had been drinking or using drugs, and that is what had caused the accident. In reconstructing the accident, it was obvious from the course the Jeep had taken that he must have blacked out. He made no attempt to follow the slow curve in the road, but instead, the Jeep had gone straight until it crashed into the only outcrop in the otherwise flat desert landscape, a five-by-eight-foot boulder. The impact caused the Jeep to roll and threw Richard and Chuck through the windshield. Chuck was trapped under the Jeep, while Richard was thrown a few feet from it. The Jeep settled in tumbleweed, and the heat of the engine and exhaust caused it to ignite. Amazingly, given they were in the middle of the desert, an Indian woman happened to be driving by and managed to pull Richard farther away from the Jeep. Chuck was not so lucky—he remained trapped under the burning vehicle. He died a few hours later at the Yosemite Burn Center.

There was no indication of drug or alcohol use in Richard's blood. The blackout was caused by what these sixteen-year-olds did not know: that the aerosol can had a warning on it to not spray the contents in an enclosed area. The warning notice said, "Intentional misuse by deliberately concentrating and inhaling the contents can be harmful or fatal." Richard and Chuck had not used it intentionally or deliberately for the purpose implied by the warning label. They had used it intentionally and deliberately for benign reasons, but the effect turned out the same: it was both harmful and fatal.

For several days, Richard was not told that Chuck had died. When a priest finally told him, he was on morphine and didn't really comprehend what had happened. Even after he was off the morphine, he didn't fully believe Chuck wouldn't reappear. He had the feeling Chuck was on vacation, which is often the way children experience death. It is difficult for them to understand the permanency of death. Even though Richard was not a young child, he was only sixteen and had never experienced the death of someone so close.

Richard was not only suffering from lung contusions, broken ribs, and cuts all over his body but also his ankle had been thoroughly shattered in the accident. The orthopedic surgeon held out little hope for Richard to have full rehabilitation. For the next two years, Richard sought out and utilized every form of surgery and physical therapy available in the United States. With all this effort, the doctors were able to save his foot, but his ability to move with ease was severely limited and he still needed a cane. He went to Switzerland, where one last operation allowed him to walk without the use of a cane. He became a physical success story.

Richard is also a psychological and spiritual success story. But as with his physical battle, he went through a prolonged internal struggle. His best friend had died in an accident in which Richard was the driver. His questions were many. What did it mean? Did it mean anything? Was it his fault? What if they hadn't sprayed the deodorant? What if they had made it to Bishop? What if it had been only two more miles, instead of forty more miles? What if? What if? What if? He realized he had a lot to think about and a lot of questions to answer. Others seemed to agree—he was plagued by his mother's pressuring him to see a psychiatrist and friends pursuing him with questioning concern. He was uncomfortable with everyone's attention and questions. He realized the questions had to be his to ask and his to answer. He had a lot of time to think, and he used the time well. Richard became a serious student of himself and of spirituality and life, feeling compelled to answer questions that most sixteen-year-olds don't even know exist.

Richard found his answers. He affirmed to himself that he was not responsible for Chuck's death and came to believe this had happened because it was meant to be. In fact, out of this experience Richard came to believe that life has a certain order to it and that everything happens for a reason. He also came to believe in an afterlife, because from the time the Jeep hit the boulder to when he woke up in the ambulance, Richard had the experience of being in a long white tunnel that had a vanishing point. He knew he was on his way to meeting people he had not seen for a while, and he looked forward to the world beyond with calm anticipation.

Richard matured quickly after the accident. He spent a great deal of the two plus years watching documentary films, providing himself an education he believed was far superior to any he had in school. From that he found his life's work as an artist and photographer. The walls of his living room are covered with his art. They are large and impressive pieces, some of them with images of death in their backgrounds, done in oils and acrylics and resins. He pursues his art and photography with fervor, as well as his *friendships with older people who think about life—who think about the big questions.*

Richard is highly motivated to live fully. And he does so with gratitude and fulfillment. He does it for himself and he does it for Chuck. Chuck's early life had not been easy and he had looked to Richard for security and with trust. In fact, Richard was one year older and like a big brother to Chuck. After the accident, Richard's deep questioning brought him to the realization that he was not responsible for Chuck's death, but that he did have a responsibility to Chuck's trust in him. He meets this responsibility by thinking about life, taking it seriously, treating it respectfully, and living it fully, for he realized that for as long as he lives, he is living for two.[1]

A General Comment

- There are times when trauma results in death. This intensifies, to a great degree, the aftermath of trauma.
- If the person who died was someone close to you and essential in your everyday life, the loss will be tremendous. But even if the person wasn't as essential to you, your trauma will be magnified by the loss.
- The death of someone often leads to particular aftereffects. These aftereffects are different in adults than in children:
  - You feel *shock* when someone unexpectedly dies, just as you feel shock after trauma.
  - If the traumatizing event includes a death, your shock will be greater and last longer.
  - During this phase, you may experience yourself feeling numb, dazed, and/or frozen. You may find yourself doing what you have always done, but in robot fashion.

- Until this phase has passed, you may not realize that you were in shock.

❧ The shock response to loss serves the same purpose as it does in reaction to trauma:
- It protects you from feeling too much.
- It helps you do what is necessary.
- It is, at this stage, your friend.

What Happens When You Lose Someone

❧ The shock will begin to wear off.

❧ In its place there may be **denial,** although shock and denial may alternate.

❧ Denial is like shock because it helps protect you from painful realities.

❧ Denial fluctuates with its opposite, **reality.** You will probably find yourself experiencing one and then the other.

❧ Reality will bring the **realization of your loss.**

❧ And with that reality you will begin to feel the **pain of your loss.**

❧ Depending on who the person was that you lost, this pain may range from mild to excruciating.

❧ For example, losing a spouse or a child may bring the worst pain, while losing someone who wasn't an integral part of your life may be less painful.

> *"In the beginning, all you want is just to die right along with your child and, after a while, as time goes by, you want to live because of that person."*[2]

❧ Along with the pain, there will be other emotions during this period.

Other Emotions and Reactions

🏵 Other emotions you may experience during this period are:
  - Isolation.
  - Anger . . .
    - At your loved one for leaving you.
    - At yourself if you think you could have prevented the death.
    - At others who you think could have prevented the death.
  - Physical distress because grief is often expressed through the body.
  - Guilt. . .
    - For acts, thoughts, or words you thought were hurtful to the person who died.
    - For not saving the person from death.
  - Depression and frequent crying.
  - An aching emptiness.

"It's the quiet times that are hard: the first waking moment of the morning when you realize that your daughter is dead."[3]

  - A wish to die.

Time Does Heal

🏵 These emotions and reactions may last for some time.

🏵 But, as the reality becomes certain, other reactions will surface.
  - You may find yourself becoming cut off from others.
    - For some, this may be a choice. You may need to be by yourself.
    - You may cut off from others because you fear they won't want to be around you, owing to your depression and unhappiness. This may be true, as people have trouble knowing how to react to someone in mourning.

- If you do not want to be alone, try to find people who can be with you. They are out there, and if they are not among your friends or families, support groups are available.

Feeling the Loss

- You may be feeling **a sense of incompleteness,** especially if you have lost a life partner, a child, a parent, or a very close friend.
- This feeling of loss may last for a long time, since it is usually impossible to fill the space created by the loss of your loved one.
- Even if you try to fill that void, you will probably find. . .
  - You just can't. It is hard to make room for someone new when you are mourning.
  - It isn't wise. You need this time to mourn your loved one so you can eventually let go.
  - The heaviness you are feeling will interfere with any positive connection with someone new.
  - You are trying to find a replacement, someone like the one you lost. But there are no replacements. The person you lost was unique, so there are no substitutes. This doesn't mean you won't have someone new, but it will be just that—someone new.

Remembering

- There may be a period where you find yourself thinking **only positive thoughts about the one you have lost.**
- This protects you from feeling uncomfortable feelings like guilt for having negative thoughts about someone who died.
- It is human to have both positive and negative thoughts about anyone with whom you are involved, whether or not they are still living.
- You may find you **talk a lot about the person.** This is another way of keeping the one you lost with you. It helps to remember.

> *"We talk about her all the time. She's always in our conversation: 'Remember when Sheila did this?' or 'Remember when she would do that?'"*[4]

- You may find yourself taking on the dress style or mannerisms or interests of the person you have lost. This is a common and helpful way of keeping that person with you for the rest of your life. However, if this is excessive or persists past a couple of years, it may be a warning sign that you are finding yourself unable to relinquish the one you have lost. You may, then, need professional help to facilitate your mourning.
- Eventually, you will find the pain lessening.
- You will also find yourself turning to others and finding new relationships. When this begins, you are starting to complete mourning.

CHAPTER TWENTY

When a Child Loses Someone

- Your child's reaction to death will depend on . . .
  - The **age** of your child.
  - **Who** the child lost.
- Children under the age of eight or nine don't understand the permanency of death.
- Instead, they experience death as if the person had left but still exists. Therefore, death to them is often felt as an **abandonment** or a punishment.
- Children are often overlooked when there is a death because the adults in their world are occupied with their own grieving. Therefore,
  - The reactions of children go unnoticed.
  - Children lack information needed to understand what has happened.
  - Children have no chance to talk about their reactions, which can lead to prolonged mourning time.
- Children may worry that the death had **something to do with them.**
  - Children see the world as emanating from within them. They believe their words, thoughts, and actions cause what happens in their world.
- When children do not have a chance to talk about their thinking about the death, they are left **believing their own fantasies.**

- For example, a child may believe Daddy died because he had a bad thought about Daddy.
- That Mommy left because she was mad about their room not being cleaned up.
- Or they are being punished because they thought or did something bad.

ª This is why it is important for children to have a chance to talk about their ideas about why they think the death occurred.

ª For children who can't talk (because they are too young or can't find the words or for any other reason), it may help to let them draw.

ª With either talking or drawing, the child can be invited to express his or her feelings. For example, a grown-up might say, "I was thinking about your Daddy just now. I wonder if you think about him?" or "Maybe we could draw a picture about you and Daddy."

NOTE: This is a book about trauma and only secondarily about loss through death. Losing someone can be a major event for an adult or a child, and you may want to read more than what is offered here (see Appendix B).

PART EIGHT

Final Thoughts

Some people are . . . unaware that reality contains unparalleled beauties. The fantastic and unexpected, the ever-changing and renewing is nowhere so exemplified as in real life itself.[1]

CHAPTER TWENTY-ONE

The Look of Recovery

"For many of the people the shock and the loss from [Hurricane] Hugo (in South Carolina) have been too great and the scars too deep to ever heal. Every time the clouds change color or the wind picks up, memories of the terrible night of the storm come back stronger than ever.... Some people still have trouble sleeping, some keep their radios on the weather station all night long, and some can't stop watching the sky and the waves and listening for the wind. And some, like a certain very thin and very old lady ... are convinced the worst is yet to come. When people stop to see the fish in her bucket she takes their arm with one hand, and turning pages with the other until she finds her place, she makes them listen to Ecclesiastes, chapter one, verse six: 'The wind goeth toward the south, and turneth unto the north; it whirleth about continually, and the wind returneth again according to His circuits.' "[1]

🔊 This woman has not yet recovered and it may be she never will.

🔊 It is a sad fact that there are people who do not recover. When people have had too many of the circumstances discussed in Chapter 13 ("Some Take Longer"), they may not recover. It is difficult to heal when the odds are overwhelming.

🔊 However, aside from some minor lingering aftereffects, **most people do recover.**

> *I have one lingering aftereffect from when I was beaten up in the riot twenty years ago. It happens when I am out walking alone. If I see two or more people walking toward me, I move to the other side of the street. If that isn't possible, I turn down a side street, even if it means going several blocks out of my way. It helps me to do this . . . I call it fear management. This seems to be my only lingering aftereffect. I feel fortunate that this is all that lingers. It seems to me it could have been much more than this, but I rarely think about The Day-I-Was-Beaten-Up-in-the-Riot. Also, I am appreciative of this aftereffect because I feel it keeps me safe by being alert. I like that I am cautious. I think it is a smart way to be.[2]*

🔊 Recovery isn't the same for everyone, and it is impossible to describe all the ways recovery looks. However, there are some general signs of recovery.

Lessened Reactions

  Most of your intense reactions will have subsided or disappeared.

- You will no longer suffer from hyperarousal.
- You will not be disturbed by nightmares and, therefore, you will sleep better.
- You won't be as easily startled by sounds or the sudden appearance of someone, and you will be less wary.
- You will no longer experience the raw emotions of terror, anger, and helplessness.

> *Ruth lived next door to a house that exploded on the second night of the Los Angeles riots. In seconds, the neighboring house was unrecognizable and there was a sixty-foot ball of fire leaping toward the sky. Ruth's fence was blown apart and her windows instantly imploded. Her house was saved from destruction only because the wind was blowing the flames away. Soon after the explosion, Ruth jumped at every sound and every rumble, sure it was going to happen again. It was almost two years later when she realized she wasn't jumping anymore. Sometimes now, if she is especially tired, she is startled like before, but it is unusual. It is a relief to feel the edginess disappear, a relief to again have periods of time when she feels like she used to feel.*[3]

- If you do notice an increase in reactions, it may be due to an **anniversary reaction.** This occurs at the same time of the year as the original trauma and usually diminishes as the years go on.

No More Denial and Intrusions

❧ Denial and intrusions will be absent from your experience.

❧ For those who suffered from alternating experiences of denial and intrusions, you will be relieved to have them in the past.

- This is especially true for intrusions that are, by definition, unwanted and quite often frightening.
- It is also a relief to be rid of denial because it so often makes you feel zombielike. It is the absence of that zombielike experience that lets you know denial has lifted.

❧ Simultaneously, you may notice your perceptions and thinking seem clearer and crisper. Now you can concentrate when before you were having trouble doing so.

❧ It's not dissimilar to the experience of having one cloudy day after another and then a day with sunshine and blue sky—what a difference it makes! Everything looks clearer, brighter, more noticeable. It is the same when denial passes.

When I interviewed Andrea three months after the Southern California earthquake, she said she thought she must be recovering, since she no longer had the sensation she was under water all the time—no longer did everything seem muffled and strange. Her shock and denial had worn off.[4]

No More Confused Questioning

 ❧ When you reach recovery, you will no longer be questioning yourself and the world in the same confused and intense way you were.
- You will probably have adopted a new world view—one where you understand that random events happen.
- You will see yourself as someone who is vulnerable to trauma. Most of us live with the denial that nothing will happen to us, and when it does we then realize we are not invincible. And once we finally know we're not invincible, we know it forever.

 ❧ What comes with recovery is a perspective on these events.
- You realize that, yes, random events do happen and, yes, they can happen to you.
- But you also realize that random events happen far less than the routine events of life, and they are **rare** occurrences in most of our lives.
- This event did not have anything to do with you personally, so that if something happens in the future, it is not about you, but about chance.

Regained Control

 ❧ You will feel more in control of your life again.
- This is a result of feeling you are able to function again the way you did before the trauma. Your everyday life is no longer interfered with by sleeplessness, anxiety, exhaustion, and poor concentration. You notice you are your old self again.
  - The feelings of being little, inadequate, and overwhelmed will mostly be gone.
  - An adult sense of yourself will be reinstated.

 ❧ Being back in control is a result of having mastered the trauma. That is, you fought back from its effects to become more like you used to be. This leaves you knowing that, in spite of how difficult it was, you were able to overcome it.

> *Mike, who had a serious auto accident, explains:*
> *"I remember that first day I went back to work.*
> *I felt like I was King of the Mountain. I knew I*
> *was a survivor and that no matter how difficult*
> *it had been to get to this point, I had done it. It*
> *was one of the highs of my life."[5]*

The Pieces Come Together

- ❧ You will feel that all the pieces of the puzzle fit together.
  - This is the result of having found a way to make sense of the event.
- ❧ You will have arrived at this point because you have taken the steps toward resolution:
  - You will have mourned.
  - You will have found the words to describe the experience.
  - You will have discovered acceptance.
  - You will have taken action and achieved self-care.
- ❧ You can tell the puzzle pieces are fitting together because you are no longer spending your time and thoughts on the trauma. You will notice that hours and then days and then weeks go by without thinking about what happened.

> *This can take quite a lot of time and under cer-*
> *tain circumstances you cannot help but think*
> *about it. For instance, Greg and his family, who*
> *were flooded out twice in the Midwest floods of*
> *1993, are still fixing things almost a year later.*
> *Greg has to think about it every day because*
> *there is still work to be done. But the day will*
> *come when the work is completed and his mind*
> *will again be filled with what it was before—this*
> *year's baseball team and his children's schooling*
> *and his job as a UPS driver.[6]*

Realized Outcomes

ᴥ More than likely, you will have realized one or more of
the outcomes that result from resolution.

- You will have realized *you* were not destroyed by
the trauma—that is, that no matter what happened
to you, you are still you. This can make you feel
triumphant.
- More than likely you will have reevaluated your
values and goals, found a new sense of compassion
for others, and perhaps taken some social action.
- You will see that you are permanently changed.

ᴥ For some, the reevaluation, compassion, and change are
minuscule. For others, like Sherry, it is immeasurable.

> *Sherry managed to look regal on the crutch she
> was using because of a calf pull. Not only did
> she look regal, she almost looked foreboding. I
> figured out later that it really is an aura that
> results from her determination—determination
> not to miss a beat, to feel every breath, not to
> waste a minute. Sherry does not give away her
> minutes anymore.*
>
> *In February, a couple of years ago, Sherry,
> her son, and her now ex-husband were driving
> from San Diego to Los Angeles. She recounts
> that in the space of one second she had a severe
> headache. She screamed and yelled, "Pull over,
> pull over." She bolted from the car, landing in
> the gravel at the roadside, on her knees, vomit-
> ing and sweating violently. "Ambulance" was
> all she could say.*
>
> *The ambulance came. She was tested at the
> hospital and discharged after being told there
> was nothing wrong, and that it was just a mi-
> graine. Sherry knew better. She knew it was*

something "right here, right behind my right eye," cupping her hand over her eye to show me the place. Sherry was sent home, but she didn't get better. She became more afraid and more tired. On the second night, she called her mother to ask her to please come over and put her son to bed later in the evening. She was too tired to stay up, even though she hadn't worked that day. (Sherry is a physical therapist who never misses a day at work.) Her mother came over and noticed Sherry was acting "strange." Her mother stayed, periodically checking on her, and at 5 A.M. she found Sherry sitting on the floor soaked in sweat. Her mother said all there was to say, "Let's go." Somehow, Sherry knew she was in a lot of trouble and knew there wasn't much time.

They rushed to the nearby hospital, a different hospital from the one before. More tests were done with the same results . . . there was no sign of anything. But this time it was decided to look further by doing an angiogram. The angiogram lasted three hours. I understand from Sherry that angiograms usually last no longer than forty-five minutes, but because after forty-five minutes they still hadn't found anything, they continued. The angiogram was excruciating. It was done without pain medication.

Sherry found a way to self-medicate. She decided not to hang around. She left. She took a little trip—about fifteen feet up to be exact. She became a three-year-old, perched on the ceiling, above what was happening below. What this three-year-old saw was a lady on a table with people doing things to her. "Look at what they are doing to that lady down there, look how they're moving her around, they shouldn't use that tape, they're going to pull her hair out." The

*three-year-old talked for as long as the angio-
gram lasted. Sherry now says about that little girl,
"I was so grateful for her. It wasn't pain in me, it
was pain in her down there, so I didn't feel it."*

*The angiogram was over and Sherry remem-
bers a sound. Neither of us is sure how to spell it,
but it's something like whmmph. It was the sound
of coming off the ceiling and back into herself.
The doctor gave her the findings, a confirmation
of what she knew all along. There was something
wrong behind her right eye. An operable aneu-
rysm—a killer behind her right eye that would
have been fatal if it had not been pressing against
the tentorium, the most pain-sensitive area of the
brain, and if it had not been located. The artery
was stretched so thin the doctor could see the
blood pulsating through. They found it just in
time. The doctor told Sherry the news and that
they would be going into surgery immediately.
Sherry involuntarily exclaimed, "Goodie." It had
to have warmed that doctor's heart.*

*Sherry is two years past the moment when she
said "goodie." But her every action repeats
goodie. It's "Goodie, I am alive." It's "Goodie, I
am ice skating" (every morning). It's "Goodie,
I am playing tennis" (every night). It's "Goodie, I
got out of a devastating marriage" (she left soon
after returning home from the hospital). It's
"Goodie, I let a man with a soft soul near me" (a
welcome change from previous choices). It's
"Goodie, I'm not giving my minutes away" (who
wants to waste their minutes getting mad at traffic?). And it's "Goodie, this year right here. This
has definitely been my favorite year" (and I live as
if it could be my last).*

*Living each year as if it could be her last is
wonderful for Sherry, but it has a double edge to
it. There is this fear, and this fear is what moti-*

vates her not to miss a minute. She says the fear is not because she is afraid to die. She feels that whatever happens she is ready to deal with it, to surrender, to let go. In fact, she says that before she went into surgery she saw herself going through an arched entryway. She thinks it was the archway to heaven. And in that moment, she let go. She says that moment was a most effective moment and is what makes her who she is today. "The deep-down core of me is relaxed about dying. I feel I know something most people don't know and that I have a gift inside of me that gives me a lot of strength to do with the loss of the fear of dying and with the joy of life. I get juice from using it. I use it every day, it's something I know, like I carry it around like a little bag of secrets. I have it no matter what. I have all the pieces."

So, if she's not afraid of dying, what is it? What causes the double edge that is wonderfulness and fear? It's the fear of not having enough minutes. That is different from the fear of dying.[7]

Epilogue

In our civilized culture where electricity abounds, we seldom have the experience of being in total darkness. There is always a light, somewhere in the night, anchoring us, guiding us. We seldom have the experience of being jolted awake, without warning, without preamble. Jolted and thrown out of bed, hearing what you are sure must be a freight train pushing through the earth under your very being . . . and then hearing crashing, breaking, banging. All this as you roll in the rough seas your home has become in the pitch black of the early morning. The lurching finally stops and there is a moment for relief. Then suddenly, inexplicably, the sky brightens just like it does on the Fourth of July. You have no idea what is making this happen, but you are appreciative of those moments because at least now you can see. You look around, but you don't recognize what you see because it isn't the way you left it the night before—or any other time, for that matter. Everything is different and nothing is distinguishable. There are just mounds of indecipherable objects. Before you have time to make sense of any of them, it suddenly is black again. You don't learn until later it was the transformers exploding that caused those quick bursts of light.

Almost simultaneous with the second round of blackness, there is that sound again, that train sound. It nearly drowns out the clanging and crashing and breaking of more of your worldly possessions. It's not over for Southern California. Those first few minutes, starting at 4:31 A.M. on January 17, 1994, were only the beginning for most and, sadly, the end for a few.

The stories are endless, the experiences are endless, and all are unique—quakes are like that. There is no uniformity. One window shatters, another does not. One lamp falls, another stands. There is no discernible path, no discernible pattern. It isn't every other building, it isn't only old buildings, it isn't just tall buildings or just low buildings, or one whole city and none of another. It is as if we each experienced something different, but something the same. As each new bizarre story is recounted in the aftermath, the shock is renewed. We each wonder, how could it be, how could it be? Our heads become thick with trying to understand one unfathomable report after another. We move with each other and past each other, looking, gawking, looking, trying to make room in our minds for the fact that on that beautiful boulevard near the beach that beautiful building is bent. How can you make room in your mind for a bent building? We know about damaged buildings, we know about demolished buildings, we know about buildings under construction and under reconstruction . . . but bent? No, we don't know about bent. And we don't know about buildings that now seem no sturdier than our young children's Lego sets.

We leave the house at dusk on that first day of the biggest quake to hit Southern California for longer than anyone can remember and we discover the jumble our world has become. It is the end of a very long day and although you would think we would want to stay home and rest from the weariness that has settled in to stay for a while, we could not. We were compelled to wrap up this day as we had led it—to be with others,

around others, to look and to see, to begin to come to terms
with that which would be with us for a very long while. We
took the main thoroughfare and within blocks I was taken
aback by the odor of gas, by the sight of flames, by the glass
under our tires, by the piles of bricks and boards and facades,
by our Mexican neighbors on the sidewalks wrapped in blan-
kets holding radios terrified to be inside (the Mexico City
quake still looms for them), by the homeless man reaching
through a broken display window to put a flower in the hand
of a tuxedo-garbed mannequin that had fallen on its side, by
the fact that I could look inside an entire building because the
front was sheared off, creating a life-size doll house.

We arrived, eventually, on the side of town where the most
damage had occurred. It seemed essential to walk these streets,
to honor them with a slow taking in, not a quick drive-by. It
was cold out, so it was difficult to walk the boulevard for long,
but it was long enough to see enough to realize it wasn't the
cold that was taking our breath away. Instead, it was the tight-
ness in our chests from tears that couldn't yet come. Our city,
once more, had been grievously injured. We had barely time to
catch our breath, but this time it truly was our collective breath
for there wasn't one of us who wasn't affected. Unlike the riots
and the fires and the floods, which remained neatly in their
enclaves, this was everywhere. It was an everybody experience.

There were many of us walking down the boulevard that
early evening. We caught each other's eyes. Our slight smiles
barely covered how aghast we were. We didn't actually speak
to each other and yet we were communicating. In each of our
minds was the chant, the chant that spread through every
Southern California mind more rapidly than the wild fires of
only a few months earlier, the chant that ignited soon after
4:31 A.M., became trite within minutes, but in spite of that
forced itself into our minds over and over and over again. I
said the chant quietly in my own mind, but every pair of eyes
I looked into during those moments at dusk knew my chant
because it was also theirs. It became our city chorus. We sang
it a cappella and in unison and it rang quietly in our heads as

loud and as grateful and as strong as anyone could imagine without ever hearing even a whisper of it out loud. Thank God it struck at 4:31 A.M., thank God it was Martin Luther King Day, thank God, thank God, thank God. Its rhythm was as sure as our footsteps on the boulevard. Our multicultural, multilingual, multifaith-nonfaith Los Angeles universe finally spoke the same language. For some hours, for some days, maybe for some infinite forever, we the citizens of this great and maligned city no longer have lines that differentiate us, for we are united in our chorus of unison.

The trauma of the earthquake was such a different experience from the one I had twenty years earlier when I was beaten up in the riot, for then I was ununited, without a unison. I was alone in a way I had never experienced. On this earthquake day, I was joined to millions. Even though we may have been going our separate ways as we left the boulevard to locate our cars to go home at dark at the end of the first day, we remained together, forever. I can't really say it was a better feeling than the one twenty years earlier, but surely I can say it was a less lonely feeling. And just seconds ago—almost five months later to the day, as I sit and write and remember— there were two aftershocks. A smile of irony touches my face. I don't think any of you will believe that my house shook— twice, just now—as the words I am writing appear on the screen. The tinkling of my mother's china was suddenly our background music, the fear in my heart our background feeling. Here I am, not only joined with every other resident of Southern California but, now, with you, my reader and fellow trauma victim. You never imagined and I never imagined we would be together in an aftershock. But that is the way trauma is—never really anticipated, never really imagined. I sit here with a certain calm. It is a calm that has grown out of having survived . . . and from that, a certain attitude develops. It's an attitude that many Southern Californians have adopted and one that almost every trauma victim comes to realize. It is the attitude captured in this recently seen T-shirt slogan:

Shifts happen.

APPENDICES

APPENDIX A

Resources for Those Seriously or Permanently Injured

Telephone Numbers

American Amputee Foundation	501-666-2523
American Council of the Blind	800-424-8666
Americans with Disabilities Act:	
Employment Helpline	800-669-8800
Technical Assistance Hotline	800-466-4ADA
National Center for Youth with	
Disabilities	800-333-6293
National Head Injury Foundation	
Family Helpline	800-444-NHIF
National Rehabilitation Information	
Center	800-34-NARIC
National Spinal Cord Injury Hotline	800-526-3456

Readings

The Consumer's Guide to Long-Term Care. External Affairs Department, American Council of Life Insurance, 1001 Pennsylvania Avenue, N.W., Washington, D.C. 20004; 202-624-2000.

Klein, R., and K. Kroll. *Enabling Romance: A Guide to Love, Sex and Relationships for the Disabled (and the People Who Care about Them)*. New York: Harmony Books, 1992; 800-773-3000.

Shapiro, J. P. *No Pity: People with Disabilities Forging a New Civil Rights Movement*. New York: Times Books, 1993; 800-773-3000.

Stolman, M. D. *A Guide to Legal Rights for People with Disabilities*. Demos Publications, 386 Park Avenue South, Suite 201, New York, New York 10016; 800-532-8663.

APPENDIX B

Additional Reading

If You Are Helping Someone Who Is Ill

Dass, R. and P. Gorman. *How Can I Help?* New York: Alfred A. Knopf, 1985.

Felder, L. *When a Loved One Is Ill: How to Take Better Care of Your Loved One, Your Family, and Yourself.* New York: Plume, Penguin Books, 1990.

Strong, M. *Mainstay: for the Well Spouse of the Chronically Ill.* Boston: Little, Brown, 1988.

For Adults Who Have Lost Someone Through Death

Grollman, E. A. *What Helped Me When My Loved One Died.* Boston: Beacon, 1981.

Levine, S. *Who Dies?* New York: Doubleday–Ancher Books, 1982.

Lewis, C. S. *A Grief Observed.* London: Faber & Faber, 1961.

Schiff, H. S. *The Bereaved Parent.* New York: Penguin, 1981.

For Children Who Have Lost Someone Through Death

Grollman, E. A., ed. *Explaining Death to Children.* Boston: Beacon Press, 1976.

Krementz, J. *How It Feels When a Parent Dies*. New York: Knopf, 1993.

Mellonie, B. and R. Ingpen. *Lifetimes*. New York: Bantam Books, 1983.

Prestine, J. S. *Helping Children Cope with Death*. Carthage, IL: Fearon Teacher Aids, 1993.

Prestine, J. S. *Someone Special Died*. Carthage, IL: Fearon Teacher Aids, 1993.

Simon, N. *The Saddest Time*. Morton Grove, IL: Albert Whitman & Co., 1986.

Viorst, J. *The Tenth Good Thing About Barney*. New York: Atheneum, 1971.

APPENDIX C

800 Numbers

General Information Line	800-339-6993
	800-333-9997
National Rehabilitation Information Center	800-346-2742
Victims of Crime Resource Center:	
Sexual Assault	800-842-8467
Legal Services	800-843-9053
U.S. Department of Health and Human Services	800-336-4797
Crisis Response Unit	800-833-3376
Suicide Prevention Hotline	800-333-4444
Youth Crisis Hotline	800-448-4663
Child Abuse Reporting Hotline	800-540-4000
Child Help USA	800-4ACHILD
Elder Abuse Hotline	800-992-1660
Central Violations Bureau	800-366-5245
National Clearinghouse on Childhood Abuse and Neglect and Family Violence Information	800-394-3366
American Trauma Society	800-556-7890
National Center for Missing and Exploited Children	800-843-5678
National Organization for Victims Assistance	800-TRY-NOVA
National Victim Center	800-FYI-CALL

APPENDIX D

Self-Help Clearinghouse Numbers

California	800-222-5465
	800-445-8106
Connecticut	800-842-1501
Illinois	800-322-MASH
Kansas	316-686-1205
Massachusetts	413-545-2313
Michigan	800-752-5858
Minnesota	612-642-4060
Missouri (West)	816-361-5007
Missouri (East)	314-371-6500
Nebraska	402-476-9668
New Jersey	800-FOR-MASH
New York City	212-840-1259
New York (Upstate)	518-474-6293
Ohio	216-762-7471
Oregon and Washington	503-222-5555
Pennsylvania	609-663-3422
	412-247-5400
	717-961-1234
South Carolina	803-791-9227
Tennessee	615-588-9747
Texas	214-871-2420
Vermont	800-554-5030
Virginia and District of Columbia	703-536-4100
Wisconsin	414-933-0428

Alberta	403-262-1117
British Columbia	604-721-8036
Ontario	416-978-3270
Quebec	514-731-8059
Saskatchewan	306-652-7817

APPENDIX E

Local Numbers

California Trial Lawyers Association 800-767-2852

Los Angeles Trial Lawyers Association 213-487-1212

Scottsdale Prevention Institute 602-994-0004

Trauma Response Center of Los Angeles County
   Contacts:
   Dr. Mariann Hybels-Steer 310-915-9205
   Dr. Diane Mink 310-826-1085

Victims of Crime Resource Center 916-739-7061

Notes

Part Two: Coming Apart in the Immediate Aftermath

1. M. Clare, "Clouds of Despair Linger in Florida in Andrew's Wake," *Los Angeles Times*, 8-23-93, A1.

Chapter Three: The Effect on Your Body and Mind

1. Interview, Andrea, 1994.
2. Interview, Mike, 1993.
3. C. H. Craft, "Robbery Victims Urge Security Bill," *Los Angeles Times*, June 13, 1993, A28.
4. "After Shocks," *Los Angeles Times*, October 17, 1990, E1.
5. Interview, Bernard Geller, M.D., Ph.D., 1994.
6. Interview, Linda, 1994.
7. M. Dolan, "Lessons of Oakland Hills Blaze," *Los Angeles Times*, October 29, 1993, A1.
8. Interview, Sally, 1993.
9. Interview, Judie, 1993.
10. Interview, Dorothy, 1993.
11. Interview, Judie, 1993.
12. Interview, Mary, 1993.
13. Interview, Andrea, 1994.
14. Interview, Jim, 1993.

Chapter Four: What Helps?

1. Interview, Andrea, 1994.
2. Interview, Dede, 1994.
3. Interview, Jim, 1993.

Part Three: The Middle Period of Disarray

1. R. M. Rilke, *Letters to a Young Poet* (New York: Vintage Books, 1986), No. 4.

Chapter Six: Denial and Intrusions

1. Interview, Mary, 1993.
2. Interview, Nancy Becker-Kennedy, 1993.
3. Interview, Kelly McGillis, 1994.
4. Interview, Shawnee, 1993.
5. Ibid.

Chapter Seven: Other Emotional Reactions

1. Interview, Andrea, 1994.
2. Interview, Judie, 1993.
3. Interview, Mary, 1993.
4. Interviews, Jim, Judie, Shawnee, 1993.
5. Interview, Kelly McGillis, 1994.

Chapter Eight: Everything Is Questioned

1. Interview, Shawnee, 1993.
2. Interview, Kelly McGillis, 1994.
3. R. Janoff-Bulman, *Shattered Assumptions* (New York: The Free Press, 1992).

Chapter Nine: The Reactions of Others

1. Interview, Tom, 1993.
2. M. Bard and D. Sangrey, *The Crime Victim's Book*, 2nd Edition (Secaucus, N.J.: Citadel Press, 1986), pp. 40–41.

3. Interview, Lynn, 1993.
4. Interview, Greg, 1994.
5. Interview, Cynthia, 1993.

Part Four: Putting It into Place via Resolution

1. Henry Wadsworth Longfellow, *Correct Quotes,* 1991, Word Star International, Inc.

Chapter Ten: Steps to Reorganization

1. Interview, Kelly McGillis, 1994.
2. Interview, Mike, 1993.
3. Interview, Gwenne, 1993.
4. Interview, Shawnee, 1993.
5. A. C. Roark, "Mending Wounds of a Massacre," *Los Angeles Times,* January 13, 1990, A1.
6. Interview, Gwenne, 1993.

Chapter Eleven: Outcomes

1. Interview, Dan, 1993.
2. Interview, Gwenne, 1993.
3. Interview, Adrian and Dede, 1994.
4. Interview, Kelly McGillis, 1994.
5. P. Carlin, "Into the Line of Fire," *Los Angeles Times,* August 13, 1991, E1.
6. Interview, Dorothy, 1993.
7. Interview, Kelly McGillis, 1994.
8. Interview, Shawnee, 1993.

Chapter Twelve: Professional Help

1. S. Roan, "America's Way of Grieving," *Los Angeles Times,* February 19, 1991, E1.

2. Interview, Kelly McGillis, 1994.
3. I. Wilkerson, "And Now, Anxiety as Terrible as the Floods," *New York Times,* September 28, 1993, 1.

Chapter Thirteen: Some Take Longer

1. Interview, Kelly McGillis, 1994.
2. Interview, Andrea, 1993.
3. Interview, Liz, 1993.
4. Interview, Kelly McGillis, 1994.

Part Five: For Those Close to Someone Traumatized

1. P. Monette, *Borrowed Time* (New York: Avon Books, 1988), 282.

Chapter Fourteen: Your Reactions

1. Interview, Betty, 1993.
2. Interview, Lynn, 1993.
3. Interview, Liz, 1993.
4. Ibid.
5. Interview, Shelly, 1993.
6. Ibid.
7. Interview, Betty, 1992.
8. R. Yglesias, *Fearless* (New York: Warner Books, 1993).

Chapter Fifteen: Helping

1. Interview, Dede, 1994.

Part Six: Traumatized Children

1. Henry Wadsworth Longfellow, *Correct Quotes,* 1991, Word Star International, Inc.

Chapter Sixteen: Common Questions

1. Interview, Ila, 1993.
2. D. S. and L. Everstine, *The Trauma Response: Treatment for Emotional Injury* (New York: W.W. Norton & Co., 1993); R. S. Pynoos and S. Eth, "Developmental Perspective on Psychic Trauma in Childhood." In *Trauma and Its Wake*, ed. by C. R. Figley (New York: Brunner/Mazel, 1985); L. Terr, *Too Scared to Cry* (New York: Harper & Row, 1990).
3. M. Hyland-Hubbard, "Crash Lasts Split Second; the Pain Goes On and On," *Los Angeles Times*.
4. Terr, *Too Scared to Cry*, 223.
5. Hyland-Hubbard, "Crash Lasts Split Second."

Chapter Seventeen: Children's Reactions

1. L. Terr, *Too Scared to Cry* (New York: Harper & Row, 1990), 270–271.
2. Ibid., 271.
3. A. C. Roark, "Mending Wounds of a Massacre," *Los Angeles Times*, January 13, 1990, A1.
4. S. Sengupta, "Slowly, Fire Victims Begin to Heal," *Los Angeles Times*, May 17, 1993, B1.
5. Interview, Greg, 1994.
6. Terr, *Too Scared to Cry*, 46–51.
7. By consent of a patient, 1993.
8. Interview, Mary, 1993.
9. Terr, *Too Scared to Cry*, 7.
10. Interview, Lynn, 1993.
11. Terr, *Too Scared to Cry*, 110.
12. These lists are compiled from my own observations along with those of D. S. Everstine and L. Everstine, *The Trauma Response: Treatment for Emotional Injury* (New York: W.W. Norton & Co., 1993); R. S. Pynoos and S. Eth, "Developmental Perspective on Psychic Trauma in Childhood." In *Trauma and Its Wake*, ed. by C. R. Figley (New York: Brunner/Mazel, 1985); Terr, *Too Scared to Cry*; "Helping Children Cope with Disaster," *American Red Cross*, ARC 4499, September 1992. I have combined the observations from all these sources in the hope of presenting the most comprehensive list possible.

13. Sengupta, "Slowly, Fire Victims Begin to Heal."
14. Interview, Mary, 1993.

Chapter Eighteen: What to Do

1. Interview, Michael, 1990.

Part Seven: When Someone Dies

1. Johann Wolfgang von Goethe, *Correct Quotes*, 1991, Word Star International, Inc.

Chapter Nineteen: When an Adult Loses Someone

1. Interview, Richard, 1994.
2. "It's the Worst Pain," *Los Angeles Times*, May 20, 1993, E1.
3. P. Carlin, "Into the Line of Fire," *Los Angeles Times*, August 13, 1991, E1.
4. "It's the Worst Pain."

Part Eight: Final Thoughts

1. B. Abbott. E. L. Beilenson and A. Tenenbaum, eds., *Wit and Wisdom of Famous American Women* (New York: Peter Pauper Press, 1986), 9.

Chapter Twenty-One: The Look of Recovery

1. W. P. Fox, *Lunatic Wind* (Chapel Hill, N.C.: Algonquin Books, 1992), 197.
2. Author's comment.
3. Interview, Ruth, 1994.
4. Interview, Andrea, 1994.
5. Interview, Mike, 1993.
6. Interview, Greg, 1994.
7. Interview, Sherry, 1993.

Index

and depression, in middle phase, 79
feeling, 206
in resolution phase, 108, 131, 134
shock response to, 203–4
See also Death
Loved ones (loss of), in resolution phase, 131

McAlexanders, the, 98
McGillis, Kelly, 66, 80, 87, 106, 122, 124, 126, 130, 138
MADD (Mothers Against Drunk Drivers), 123
Making words, in resolution phase, 107, 110
Manning, Lynn, 95–98, 146, 182–83
Martinez, Cataline, 178
Massacres, 113–14
Mastering trauma, 185, 217
Meaning
  and perception of event, in middle phase, 70
  questioning, in middle phase, 85, 89
  and social action, in resolution phase, 123
Medical attention (as basic step for action), in immediate aftermath, 48
Medication, 50, 53, 54, 68, 80
Medication consultation, in resolution phase, 128–29
Memories
  and flashbacks, 66
  intrusions as, 66
Memory
  initial impact on, in immediate aftermath, 43–44
  and shock, in immediate aftermath, 33
  See also Traumatic memory
Menstrual cycle, 32
Middle phase, 55, 57–101
  denial in, 59–64, 65, 70
  emotional reactions in, 71–80
  and immediate aftermath, 57
  intrusions in, 59, 65–70
  length of, 57
  others' reactions in, 90–101
  physical injury and, 58

preliminary thoughts on, 57–58
psychological recovery in, 58
questioning in, 81–89
and resolution phase, 57
Midwest floods, 98, 127, 218
Migraines, 32
Mind, in immediate aftermath, 33–45
  confusion, 35–36
  denial, 34
  disbelief, 35
  disorientation, 35–36
  dreams, initial impact on, 44–45
  emotions, initial impact on, 33–34
  forgetfulness, 44
  memory, initial impact on, 43–44
  perceptions, impact on, 38–43
  shock, impact of, 27–28, 33
  thinking, initial impact on, 35–37
  traumatic memory, 43
  unwanted thoughts, 36–37
  See also Psyche
Minimizing experience, in middle phase, 95
Minimizing loss, of someone traumatized, 162
Mobility, and physical-change factor, 133
Mood swings, as aftereffect, raw emotional, 71, 75–76
Mortality
  and compassion, in resolution phase, 123
  realizing, in middle phase, 73
Mothers Against Drunk Drivers. *See* MADD
Mourning, 107
  and acceptance, in resolution phase, 111
  and depression, in middle phase, 80
  importance of, in resolution phase, 108–9
  on losing someone, 206, 207
  See also I have lost, but I am
Mugging, 73, 77, 125
Mundane fears, of children, 179

Natural disasters, 41, 49, 93, 114, 133, 195
  See also Earthquakes; Floods; Hurricanes; Tornadoes

feelings about, 126–27
future, preparing children for,
193–96
group, 156
individual, 156
integration of, 105, 107
and intrusions, attempting to
confront through, 69
"and just forget about it" attitude,
126
long-term, 174
and making words, 110
mastering, 185, 217
nature of, 112
one-time, 21, 22, 172, 174
physical injury complicates, 28
putting in perspective, 126
reactions during, 45–46
reality of, 111
recovery parallels, 57
reexperiencing, 69
reminders of, leading to physical
reactions, 29
repetitive, 21
responsibility in, assessment of,
112
review after, 45–47, 54
vs. stress, 23
sudden, 21, 22
taking over everything, 153
talking about, 126
victimizing others during, 137
victims, 154
way you reacted during, 137
when person causes, 132
who you were before, 134
See also Event(s); Prior-trauma
factor
Traumatic dreams, 44–45
different forms of, 44
disguise of, 44
disturbing, 45
helpfulness of, 45
Traumatic memory
distinctness of, 43
emotional intensity of, 43
Traumatic reactions, in normal
people, 24
Traumatization
chosen for, 132
and evil in world, 132

and stereotyping, 132
as stigma, 132
and trust, breakdown in, 132
Traumatized
and blaming you, 93
helping someone, 155–64
as label, 24
not crazy, 24
reactions to someone, 141–54,
157–58
See also Retraumatized state
Trust, breakdown in, in resolution
phase, 132
Trying-to-explain-why-this-happened
reaction, to someone
traumatized, 145, 147

Unconscious
and confusion, 68
and denial, 59
Unwanted thoughts, in immediate
aftermath, 36–37
Upset state, of someone traumatized,
162

Values, and goals, reevaluating, 120,
122
Verbal children, vs. preverbal
children, 174
Victim(s)
criminal, 106
identity and status as secondary
gain, 138
invisibility felt by, 154
of natural disasters, 106
Victimizing others, during trauma,
137
Viruses, 32
Vulnerability
of children, 186
and compassion, in resolution
phase, 123
denied by blaming someone
traumatized, 151
and recovery, 217
and self-defense, in resolution
phase, 120
See also Invulnerable

Wages, restitution for lost, 152
Wayne, John, 64